REGNUM STUDIES IN MISSION

Complexities of Theologies of Wealth and Prosperity: Africa in Focus

Series Preface

Regnum Studies in Mission are born from the lived experience of Christians and Christian communities in mission, especially but not solely in the fast growing churches among the people of the developing world. These churches have more to tell than stories of growth. They are making significant impacts on their cultures in the cause of Christ They are producing 'cultural products' which express the reality of Christian faith, hope and love in their societies.

Regnum Studies in Mission are the fruit often of rigorous research to the highest international standards and always of authentic Christian engagement in the transformation of people and societies. These are for the world. The formation of Christian theology, missiology and practice in the twenty-first century will depend to a great extent on the active participation of growing churches contributing biblical and culturally appropriate expressions of Christian practice to inform World Christianity.

Regnum is supported by the generosity of EMW

Complexities of Theologies of Wealth and Prosperity: Africa in Focus

Bosela E Eale and Njoroge J Ngige

Copyright © AACC, 2022

First published 2022 by Regnum Books International

Regnum is an imprint of the Oxford Centre for Mission Studies
St. Philip and St. James Church
Woodstock Road
Oxford OX2 6HR, UK
www.ocms.ac.uk/regnum

09 08 07 06 05 04 03 7 6 5 4 3 2 1

The rights of Bosela E Eale and Njoroge J Ngige to be identified as the Editors of this Work has been asserted by them in accordance with the Copyright, Designs and Patents Act 1988.

All rights reserved. No part of this publication may be reproduced, stored in a retrieval system, or transmitted in any form or by any means, electric, mechanical, photocopying, recording or otherwise, without the prior permission of the publisher or a licence permitting restricted copying. In the UK such licences are issued by the Copyright Licensing Agency,
90 Tottenham Court Road, London W1P 9HE.

British Library Cataloguing in Publication Data
A catalogue record for this book is available from the British Library

ISBN: 978-1-5064-9726-6
eBook ISBN: 978-1-5064-9727-3

Typeset by Words by Design

Cover photo by Josh Appel on www.unsplash.com

Distributed by Fortress Press in the US, Canada, India, and Brazil

AACC-CETA

Contents

Introduction 1

PART ONE
THE CHALLENGE OF WEALTH AND PROSPERITY IN AFRICA

Complexities of Theologies of Wealth and Prosperity
Fidon R. Mwombeki 9

Trending Facets of Wealth and Prosperity Gospel in Kenya
Joseph Mutei 21

Theological Impact of Wealth and Prosperity Gospel in Tanzania
Mary L. Kategile 29

Prosperity Gospel and its Effects on the Youth in Ethiopia
Tsegahun Assefa Adugna 39

PART TWO:
BIBLICAL AND THEOLOGICAL REFLECTION ON WEALTH AND PROSPERITY IN AFRICA

Divine Blessing in Deuteronomy 28:15
Nicodeme Alagbada 53

Positive Relationship between Economics and Theology
Abednego Nkamuhabwa Keshomshahara 63

A Theological Response to the Ecological Crisis, Wealth and Prosperity
Frouisou Samuel 75

Theological Views and Intentions of Wealth and Prosperity in Modern Africa
Sekenwa Moses Briska 91

PART THREE
ECCLESIOLOGICAL RESPONSES TO WEALTH AND PROSPERITY IN AFRICA

Ecclesiological Responses to Preaching of Prosperity
Christopher Aigbadumah   107

Christianity, Poverty and Wealth in the 21st Century Church in Africa
Modest Pesha   121

Effects of Covid-19 on Wealth and Prosperity in Africa
Kwabena Asamoah-Gyadu   125

Bibliography   137

Acknowledgements

After the 1st Theological Symposium on Misleading Theologies held in Nairobi, Kenya from October 23rd to 27th 2019, which opened the way to a series of Misleading Theologies Symposia with different themes, AACC continues to promote relevant, proper and contextual theology. This book is the result of the Second Symposium on Misleading Theologies held from November 23rd to 27, 2020 with the theme "Complexities of Theologies of Wealth and Prosperity". We wish to thank all the contributors who worked hard during the difficult time of Covid-19 to prepare their papers for presentation at the symposium. This programme has been made possible by generous contributions from almost all participants who were ready to contribute at least something according to their abilities and contexts. We thank all of them. We are grateful to the World Council of Churches, Mission 21, and Kirk in Actie for their efforts to support financially Misleading Theologies Symposia without which we could not have published this book. We remain indebted to Regnum Books and all who have contributed to the publication of this book. May all find here the expression of our profound gratitude.

The Editors

Foreword

Since 2019, the All Africa Conference of Churches (AACC) started the implementation of its 2019-2023 strategy. One of the thematic areas for Theology, Interfaith Relations and Ecclesial Leadership Development programme is "Addressing Misleading Theologies." It is from that perspective that AACC engages church leaders in identifying, analysing and deconstructing misleading theologies in the continent, to counter their destructive effects on the population.

AACC is engaged in a series of Annual Symposia on Misleading Theologies at the Desmond Tutu Conference Centre and Hotel in Nairobi, Kenya. Partners, scholars, pastors and lay leaders from AACC member churches across the continent and beyond gather to discuss a particular theme related to misleading theologies chosen after the preceding symposium.

The AACC convened its 1st Theological Symposium on Misleading Theologies in October 2019, where the focus was on "Addressing Misleading Theologies in Africa." The result of the Symposium was the publication of the book: "Addressing Contextual Misleading Theologies in Africa Today", eds. Bosela E, Eale and Njoroge J. Ngige. Oxford: Regnum Books International, 2020.

The 2nd Symposium on Misleading Theologies, which focused on the theme, "Complexities of Theologies of Wealth and Prosperity," was held in November 2020 with only 66 participants due to the restrictions imposed by the Covid-19 pandemic. The result of this Symposium is this book: "Complexities of Theologies of Wealth and Prosperity."

The book offers an interesting interpretation of wealth and prosperity from different perspectives. We had remarkable presentations, demonstrating how wealth and prosperity can be used positively and negatively in our theological interpretations. Wealth and prosperity are not only God's gift, but also are often used negatively to oppress and mislead people.

I wish to thank all the contributors who worked hard during the difficult time of Covid-19, to prepare their papers for presentation at the Symposium.

It is my sincere hope that the reading of these articles will inspire us to continue conversations around the topic, shying away from both the glorification and demonization of wealth and prosperity as the results of our relationship with God. I hope our churches will embrace wealth and prosperity, encouraging people to really work for wealth creation, but always in an ethical, responsible and sustainable manner.

Fidon R. Mwombeki, Ph.D.
AACC General Secretary

Introduction
John Ngige Njoroge

The All Africa Conference of Churches (AACC) through its Department of Theology, Interfaith Relations and Ecclesial Leadership Development held the 2nd Theological Symposium on Misleading Theologies with the theme 'Complexities of Theologies of Wealth and Prosperity' from 23rd-27th November, 2020 at Desmond Tutu Conference Center in Nairobi, Kenya. The AACC, through a series of annual symposia, has purposively decided to accompany member churches in promoting relevant contextual theology in key thematic areas. It has been noticed with concern the emergence and surge in theologies that could be classified as misleading on the continent of Africa. Such misleading theologies undermine the sovereignty of Christ, fundamental biblical doctrines and sound theological ethos, and finally explain and violate the God-given dignity of vulnerable Christians. Furthermore, the harm that the misleading theologies have caused through harmful beliefs and practices to the innocent believers in the hands of quack and commercial preachers who capitalize on their innocence and vulnerability needs to be addressed.

The Symposium involved church leaders, theologians and more importantly women and youth who are the most vulnerable consumers of these misleading theologies. Those involved constructively engaged in analysing the theology of natural abundance in the context of wealth and prosperity through paper presentations, plenary discussions and working groups. The proceedings of this symposium have contributed to the production of this book, *Addressing Contextual Misleading Theologies in Africa Today*: *Complexities of Theologies of Wealth and Prosperity*.

This book is a collection of articles presented during the Symposium addressing complexities of theologies of wealth and prosperity from different theological perspectives. The main perspectives included wealth and prosperity in the context of Christian faith, such as the preaching of a prosperity gospel, biblical and theological reflections on wealth and prosperity, and church responses to issues of wealth and prosperity, poverty and the effect of Covid-19 in Africa today. This book is limited within the scope in which the Symposium's papers were presented. Therefore not all areas pertaining to theologies of wealth and prosperity are covered. This would suggest further studies in areas of the historical development of the wealth and prosperity gospel in Africa, and the theological limitations and challenges of wealth and prosperity gospel.

This is the second AACC-CETA book, thematically organized to Addressing Contextual Misleading Theologies in Africa with a special focus on *Complexities of Theologies of Wealth and Prosperity*. Further, the theme on Complexities of Theologies of Wealth and Prosperity has been divided into thematic topics. Each thematic topic addresses a specific aspect of the theologies of wealth and prosperity. The thematic topics are addressed in Parts One, Two and Three in this book. It is noted that AACC-CETA continues to hold a series of annual theological symposia addressing different challenges and aspects of contextual misleading theologies.

Part One introduces the complexities of theologies of wealth and prosperity. The main focus is on the *Complexities of Theologies of Wealth and Prosperity* as practised in Africa and how they tend to be misleading. In this part, the complexities of wealth and prosperity is identified as a lucrative enterprise in Africa wherein the church needs to responsibly engage. In order to do so, it has been proposed to have an African theology that a) promotes success and prosperity, b) recognizes that being a true Christian makes one's life prosperous, c) does not promote poverty as a sign of God in one's life, d) teaches one's relationship with God can be improved by working hard, and e), faithful and generous giving to God automatically brings prosperity as commonly used by the prosperity preachers who quote Malachi 3:10; John 10:10; Luke 17:9; Mark 9:29; Acts 5:1-11 and 2 Cor. 8:9. It is unbiblical to establish a working formula for God because He is unpredictable and paradoxical. There is no formula through which one can basically manipulate God. "If you do this...God does this!" If you give more God gives you more. If you repent your sins, God blesses you materially. Alternatively, it would be rather crucial to view a theology of blessing as a positive aspect of a prosperity gospel. A theology of blessing would be critical in promoting a paradigm shift from the theology of poverty eradication to a theology of wealth creation.

Within this part, the trending facets of wealth and prosperity gospel as practised in Kenya have been articulated. A prosperity gospel is not evil if it addresses philanthropic concerns such as generosity, charity, and benevolence as a way for building the Kingdom of God. In Kenya, a prosperity gospel has become problematic when supporting scriptures are interpreted out of context leading to the manipulation of the people of God. Most of the misinterpreted scriptural passages by the prosperity gospel preachers are John 10:10; Deut. 8:18 and Galatians 3:13; 6:7 and 1 Chron. 16:22. Within the same part, the theological impact of the intricacy of wealth of prosperity gospel as preached in Tanzania is presented. The preaching of a prosperity gospel emerged among the Pentecostal movement in Tanzania. A prosperity gospel thrives on a misinterpretation of the scripture, commercialized preaching, and an imbalanced application of the scriptures. This kind of intricacy of the prosperity gospel is not meeting the threshold of the entire biblical message of Christ on salvation and redemption. Finally, this part presents the effect of wealth and prosperity on youth in the Ethiopian Evangelical Church Makane

Yesus. In the context of the Ethiopian Evangelical Church Makane Yesus, youths are introduced to the prosperity gospel as they seek for spirituality and technology. It has been proposed that by embracing leadership, it develops an effective youth ministry, boosts the use of media and initiates microfinance systems to help the youth engage in economic enterprise that will restrain the youth from manipulative misleading theologies.

Part Two articulates the biblical and theological reflection on wealth and prosperity. Both the Old and New Testaments have theological foundations of wealth and prosperity. Likewise, the scriptures are fundamentally quoted as well as misinterpreted on issues of wealth and prosperity. This has been articulated by evaluating the relationship between divine blessing and the possession of riches by theologically reflecting on Deuteronomy 28: 15. Theological reflections on Deuteronomy 28: 15 propose that obedience is a pillar of the Christian faith, which should not be reduced to a mere determining factor of materialism. Faith, which is obedience, precedes material blessing. Material blessing is in the prerogative of God, wherefore material wealth should not be used to measure one's closeness to God. The article concludes by suggesting proper and intentional hermeneutical principles be put in place to enhance the acquisition of the intended meaning of God behind the author's writing, whereby the divine blessings promised to the people of Israel if they obey the voice of God, namely pre-eminence among the nations, material prosperity, fruitfulness, soil fertility, abundance of crops, victory in battle and success in international trade, consist in strengthening the covenant that God made with these people. Departing from this understanding of the purposes of divine blessings, prosperity theology, presented as a teaching based on the possession of wealth such as the acquisition of money and material goods, cannot fail to have a negative influence on genuine Christian faith.

In addition, this part reflects on the positive relationship between economics and theology. This is from the fact that material poverty is a challenge to most African Christians. The gospel of prosperity is understood to fill this gap by spiritualizing poverty and wealth at the same time. The relationship between theology and economic well-being, riches and blessings is understood as an indicator of one's faith in God. It has been observed that African churches are ministering in theological challenging contexts of complexities of poverty, wealth and prosperity. It is argued that while, on one hand, poverty is glorified as a precondition of inheriting the Kingdom of God, on the other hand, wealth is perceived as a product of faith or a sign of securing eternity. This part identifies elements of misleading theologies, namely the spiritualization of material poverty, and the glorification of wealth as an indication of quantified faith, or salvation. The author proposes that wealth be seen as a means to an end as opposed to it being an end in itself. This perspective will enable Africans to view wealth as a means to accomplishing the mission of God, and will also necessitate a cordial relationship between the rich and the poor in the process of eradicating poverty through wealth creation.

Furthermore, this part articulates the critical issue of ecological crisis and gives a theological response to the ecological crisis in relation to wealth and prosperity in Africa today. The article reiterates the reality and effect of the ecological crisis on human life in relation to the environment. The author identifies the ecological crisis in terms of a disconnect between theology and the environment, a lack of understanding on environmental matters and an urgent quest for materialism that has forfeited the need for an ecological balance. It is further argued that the church and the government have an ecological responsibility in relation to issues of population, the creation of wealth and the protection of the environment to facilitate the wellbeing of the creation of God. The creation of God is an "icon" of God's presence and this calls African Christians to employ the Lord's Prayer as a liturgical framework to request our daily bread which is broken and share it with others in terms of the worldwide *diakonia*.

The last section of Part Two presents theological views and the intentions of wealth and prosperity in modern Africa. It is asserted that prosperity is in the Bible and is as old as the creation of humanity (Gen. 1:26-31; 2:15-16). In addition, wealth should be possessed and used wisely. It is alluded that the notion of prosperity stemmed from the emergence of the Pentecostal Charismatic movement in the world, with Africa as its main focus and consumer at the same time. Wealth in this context connotes material possession that makes an individual acquire a massive influence as an indication of comfort and prosperity.

Part Three presents thematic topics on the churches' response to issues of wealth and prosperity in Africa. This part highlights how the preaching of the prosperity gospel is greatly affecting the ecclesial landscape of the African church today. Misleading theologies of wealth and prosperity within the ecclesial boundaries of the church has been addressed in the section under the ecclesiological response to the modern preaching of a prosperity gospel in an African context. This section expresses a historical concern for the church in Africa for having gone through a series of contentious issues that has led to heresies. Some of the issues are poverty, the glorification of the wealthy and the influential personalities in the society, commercialized politics and flamboyant lifestyles and increased corruption. It is argued that a prosperity and wealth gospel is rooted in the belief that God's will is actualized through developing faith, positive speech and donations that attract materialism.

Further, this part presents a critical view on Christianity, poverty and wealth in 21st century Africa. Wealth has been defined as having monetary and material possessions, while poverty refers to collective conditions that prevent human beings from flourishing and attaining material fulfillment. The article underlines the importance and value of human life and material possessions in regard to the African socio-economic system. The present cyclical poverty experienced in Africa is attributed to the lack of an integration between everyday life in economic affairs and faith. It has been observed that the notion of poverty is more of a mental conviction that needs to be dealt with rather than it being a reality. The deconstruction of this mentality is a human-centred development process that has to be undertaken through the mobilization of potential relationships and resources towards wealth creation.

Finally, this part examines the effects of Covid-19 on wealth and prosperity in Africa. The article gives an interrogative perspective of the health-and-wealth gospel, proposing the need for a theology of wealth and prosperity against the backdrop of the biblical phenomenological lockdowns in both the Old Testament and the New Testament. It has been observed how the corona virus pandemic has brought a change in prosperity theology rooted in the public expression of faith, the artistic choice of catchy statements, physical structures, revival meetings and flamboyant lifestyles. It has been argued that the Covid-19 pandemic has challenged the faith and the general way of doing ministry and thus called on the church to rethink ways that will enable it to survive in the post-pandemic community.

PART ONE

The Challenge of Wealth and Prosperity in Africa

Complexities of Theologies of Wealth and Prosperity
Fidon R. Mwombeki

What is wrong with wealth and prosperity? Why are there complexities in our theology on the matter? This is the Second Symposium on Misleading Theologies which the All Africa Conference of Churches (AACC) has prepared. The AACC has identified misleading theologies as a very significant issue to which churches need to pay attention in earnest, as we strive to exchange our theological insights and experiences across the continent. I am honoured to give this keynote address. And because it is an address, I will try not to be too academic, but have a solid theological foundation from experiences in Africa.

The nature of the symposia we plan to be holding annually is that of a solid theological foundation but demonstrably contextual, dealing with experiences not only in university classrooms but mainly in the so called "popular theology." We are confronted daily with popular theology in congregations by different preachers, in the popular gospel music we hear on the streets, and in public buses in our cities, in radio talk-shows across the continent, in the popular TV broadcasts in our cities and across the continent and the world. We now have very prominently the quickly and broadly shared social media clips and online personal digital channels which people in Africa access, mostly on their mobile phones. In our churches there are emerging theologies propagated freely by different "ministries" and self-proclaimed teachers, prophets, apostles, or any other ostentatious title even to members of mainline churches. What do our people hear, know, and commit to? From our First Symposium, a number of clusters of issues were identified as having misleading theologies: wealth and poverty, power and authority, health and healing, and government regulation. For the Second Symposium, we chose the issues around wealth and prosperity to start with, since they are seen to be the most ubiquitous and perverse in Africa. There is no church or religion which is not confronted by the different complexities of theologies around wealth, poverty and prosperity.

In 2010, as part of the Edinburgh 2010 series, I published an article: "The Theology of Blessing in Missionary Preaching."[1] As I was contemplating this Symposium, I thought this essay provides a foundation for this keynote

---

[1] Fidon R. Mwombeki, "The Theology of Blessing in Missionary Preaching." In *Mission Continues: Global Impulses for the 21st Century,"* ed. Claudia Waehrisch-Oblau and Fidon Mwombeki, Regnum Edinburgh 2010 Series vol. 4. Oxford: Regnum Books International, 2010, pp. 51-61.

address, as the issue is almost the same. I, therefore, allow myself to use the bulk of material in that publication easily, freely and extensively, and I apologize if I sound repetitive for those who have already read it.

In that essay I based my presentation on Luther's distinction between the "theology of the cross" and the "theology of glory" and I made three arguments:

> First, that the "theology of glory", in so far as it is understood to propagate prosperity or success as a result of faith and faithfulness to God is wrong in missionary preaching. Second, that the "theology of the cross", in so far as it is understood as accommodating suffering and poverty as signs of the presence of God, and, therefore the right situation for believers to be in, is also wrong in missionary preaching. Third, that instead of the two juxtaposed theologies, a "theology of blessing" provides a key to a correct and balanced approach in missionary preaching, whereby missionary preaching brings good news to both those who are prosperous and those who are not.[2]

In the current presentation, I will not embark on my argument about the "theology of blessing," but I will focus on the complexities we experience in our theological enterprise. My task now is to highlight these complexities and let the Symposium and afterwards the theologians in the continent continue discussing and addressing these issues.

There was a very popular TV show in America called "Who wants to be a millionaire?" Is there anyone among us who is surprised that it was popular? The answer is very clear: everyone. Even though there is a fine difference between wealth and prosperity, the two are interlinked. You can prosper without being wealthy and you can have wealth without being prosperous. Prosperity encompasses broader areas than wealth, even though many times we see wealth as prosperity. For example, there are prosperous people, including academicians and politicians, who are in effect not wealthy. For that reason, I will continue using the term prosperity to mean both.

Prosperity is defined as "a successful, flourishing, or thriving condition, especially in financial respects; good fortune."[3] Or, "a situation in which people are successful and have a lot of money."[4] So, why is the prosperity theology controversial if all of us want to prosper? Where is the complexity?

The first side of prosperity is that it is really good. We all want to prosper. We want to be healthy and wealthy. We want to live well and build decent, modern houses. We want our children to have the highest education and financial independence, and show benevolence to others. We want members of our congregations to have wealth and give to our churches generously, and have political positions so that we can see them whenever we want. Our

---

[2] Ibid., p. 51
[3] https://www.dictionary.com/browse/prosperity
[4] https://dictionary.cambridge.org/dictionary/english/prosperity

churches try what they can to make sure their leaders dress well, drive reputable vehicles, have cash to donate on fundraising events, and be able to provide hospitality at a high level. We like it when we are invited to be with the ones we consider prosperous and successful, in particular politicians and business people. Our church leaders tread carefully with authorities in order to be accorded honour, such as to travel on diplomatic passports, which conveys to them the sense of being important or successful.

I once did a simple observation or survey in my church in Tanzania, to find the overarching factor in electing church elders in congregations. My finding was that spirituality, attendance at church, being a prayer warrior, with a spirit of service to others, and such spiritual virtues unfortunately play a very minimal or secondary role. Congregations tend to elect those among themselves who are perceived to be prosperous, and are at a comparatively economically higher level. Some who are elected may not even meet the proclaimed moral standard of the congregation, but they are still elected. Pastors would like their congregations to live without financial pressures by having the congregation members who have financial means and are ready to give. That is why most of them are elected leaders of their congregations, and pastors would not like to antagonize them unnecessarily because the ministry of the congregation needs the money from these people. Pastors are jubilant and grateful when a wealthy member of the congregation comes to give a testimony, that she is bringing a cash offering because God has given him or her success in her business. Pastors normally do not trouble themselves to check whether or not that success is actually from God or from a corrupt action. The pastor thanks God with the parishioner, and makes sure others know it so that they are encouraged, even urged, to do the same. I think most pastors do earnestly believe God has had something to do with their success. So the tradition and theology around "thanksgiving" in the form of monetary donations in church is ubiquitous.

The question is, are we wrong in doing this? Is prosperity bad? Are churches wrong when they compete on which builds a more ostentatious sanctuary? Is it wrong, per se, to buy a pastor a 'posh' new car or to raise the salary of church workers? Is it really not what we would want? How does the interpretation of the commandment of loving your neighbour as yourself play out here: "Do to others what you would want them to do to you?" But at the same time, as we shall see below, the question lingers around, how much is success, and how much is simply too much? Is it appropriate to actually pressurize the congregation of mainly poor people to finance an ostentatious life for the pastor who claims to deserve it, so that they can see how good God is?

Poverty

It is not possible to discuss wealth without saying something about poverty and suffering, the antithesis. Poverty denotes basically two meanings: a lack of economic resources and material goods, as well as political and legal powerlessness and oppression. In the Bible, the poor constituted a "diverse body of social workers, beggars, debt slaves, village dwellers." There are different connotations. For example, in Proverbs, the *dal* is a lazy person, whereas for the prophets, the *dal* is an object of exploitation. But in any case, poverty is a decisive issue in the prophetic and legal traditions, which show the harsh living conditions of the poor: hunger and thirst, homelessness, exploitation, legal injustice, a lack of land. The prophets and Job protest against the oppression of the poor by the rulers. The legal texts seek to ensure social well-being of the poor through the redistribution of wealth and restrictions regarding slave labour, all intended to ease the burdens of the poor. The liturgical traditions (Psalms) offer prayers on their behalf (those praying not representing themselves as among the poor), and present a God who assists the poor in their distress. In the book of Proverbs, to the wise, poverty is either a result of laziness, or a result of God's judgment.

In the NT books, the words *ptochos, hysterematos, endees, chreia* generally connote "persons and groups lacking (totally or in some degree), the necessities of life: food, drink, clothing, shelter, health, land/employment, freedom, dignity and honour." There is considerable diversity in the NT. Any attempts to harmonize the NT teaching, and draw general conclusions to defend the "Christian virtue of capitalism", or socialism/communism, or liberation theologies, are problematic.

With the complexity of biblical evidence on poverty, it would suffice to posit that poverty is an issue that is treated extensively in the Bible, and that poverty is a reality in a society, whether Christian or not. It is undesired, but it has never gone away. There is, to our disappointment, no definitive call to end poverty! What does it mean when Jesus said in Mark 14:7, "For you always have the poor with you, and you can show kindness to them whenever you wish; but you will not always have me". Worse, the Bible speaks "about" the poor, and "for" the poor, which might imply that the subjects of the message, the protagonists, are not poor themselves. Is the Bible the book "for" the poor? God seems to tell the people to be mindful of the poor, not to treat them unjustly because somehow God is on their side and fights for them.

Misleading Theological Theses of Prosperity and Poverty

Why and when is prosperity theology misleading if indeed prosperity itself is good and desired? It is important to have a theology of prosperity in every church because it is a pertinent issue which people keep on talking about, and which concerns their daily lives. There have been different theologies of prosperity since the beginning of the church, even in the Bible, even though it is not my task now to explore these. They range from the prosperity as enormous as Solomon's, to the asceticism practised by John the Baptist and earlier prophets.

We are concerned about prosperity theology because it deals with the question of how prosperity or success, and conversely poverty and suffering, are linked with God. Is everything predestined by God? What role does the faith of an individual play to end up wealthy or poor? How should theology link worldly success and wealth with faith? Should we be calling people to repentance and to come to faith in God with the promise to be endowed with prosperity? How should we explain then the reality of poverty among many believers around the world? Truly, problematic prosperity theology has spread the world over, with its crafty use of modern media, proclaiming the good news that faith in Jesus solves all the problems in the world for the believer. It propagates that faith in Christ and obedience to some prescribed biblical practices (e.g. fasting, tithing, praying harder and longer), determine the believers' financial security, physical well-being, professional progress, and modern lifestyle. Poverty, illness, death, joblessness, childlessness, are not the will of God; they should be a matter of the past when one comes to Jesus and practises what one is told in the church by the charismatic leader. I would like to mention a few theses of prosperity theology which I find problematic.

"Any theology which promotes success and prosperity is misleading"

In my paper in 2010, I discussed what I called the "theology of the cross", where as a Lutheran myself, I have problems of how people use Luther's doctrinal position as a way to understand the revelation of God to humans, and to project it on our ordinary lives concerning suffering and poverty. I have been part of the ecumenical movement for many years, and I know how we dislike "prosperity theology", and even see it as evil. We talk so much about hardships, injustices, evil world, that we are almost never thankful for success or prosperity of any kind. The prayers common in the ecumenical movement are mostly those of lament, repentance, protest and complaint. It is very seldom to hear prayers of praise and thanksgiving.

We are normally skeptical about any proclamation of success and blessings, and when we do recognize how much we are blessed, we put a caveat on how many others are still suffering and, therefore, we, like God, "suffer with them". While we claim to be on the side of the poor, we seldom have good news for the poor, apart from declaring our solidarity with them, or somehow being on their side. Of course, good news for the poor and suffering is only about them overcoming or getting out of poverty and overcoming suffering, not simply telling them God is suffering with them. Someone told me, "I do not need a God who joins me in a terrible situation and cries with me, but a God who delivers me and takes me away from this situation".

I have always been against a theology which sometimes leads to glorifying suffering and poverty as virtues of believers.[5] I have argued that there is enough biblical evidence, as well as mission historical evidence, that God is not only God of the poor but of all. When God blesses people, many times blessings have material or financial manifestations. We should, therefore, never condemn a preacher or a theology because one preaches about the goodness of prosperity, and that God is interested in people's success in life here and now. We pray for them and work with them, so that God actually does something somehow to change their situation. There is nothing intrinsically wrong with those who are wealthy and healthy, who should be encouraged to thank God.

It is time for the ecumenical movement to find an appropriate theology, biblically based, which is positive to life in this world and praises God for prosperity. We should have good news for the "rich" as well as the poor. Our "poor focused" or "pro-poor" theology does not work in our congregations and even in the lives of our theologians who increasingly love good life and success.

Nevertheless, we need to pay serious attention to the misleading theses of prosperity theologies, particularly on the following, which I presented in my 2020 paper.[6]

"Being a true Christian makes your life prosperous"

Poverty, disease, and lack of progress are problems that people should believe in God in order to eliminate. Come to Jesus because in Jesus there is no poverty, no disease, and no failure because Jesus on the cross has overcome the world. The Bible is clear about these promises, which were promised to Israel as they moved into the Holy Land, which is supposedly the promise for us as well who believe. Many biblical promises to Israel, into the land of milk and honey, making God's people prosperous, are carefully chosen and proclaimed as being ours today. Moreover, Jesus himself said he has come so that people who believe in him should have "life in abundance," (John 10:10). All the sick people who were brought to Jesus were healed, and he continues to heal. Nothing is impossible, if necessary, with prayer and fasting, and every problem is overcome. Therefore, if you are not prosperous, there is something wrong somewhere.This is a very dangerous thesis because it is blindly one-sided. While it is true that these promises are given, it is also true that poverty is a reality which exists even among the people of God. It is also true by experience that faith does not simply eliminate these vices.

---

[5] See Fidon Mwombeki, "The Theology of the Cross: Does it make sense to Africa?" In Nils Henrik Gregsen (ed.) *The Gift of Grace*. Minneapolis, MN: Fortress Press, 2005.
[6] I reproduce most of the material from that paper, but with some additions and some modifications.

"Prosperity is a sign that God is in your life"

How do you know who is a really good believer? See their lives, by their fruits. You can tell God is in your life if all your prayers are answered, and if you make progress. Why not? That means, if you continue living in poverty, if you have illnesses that even the church has prayed for many times but you do not get healed, if your children do not get good grades at school, if you are passed over for a promotion at work, if your business runs a loss, there must be something wrong between you and God. Your faith may not be sufficient. Your prayers have elements of unbelief, or you have a hidden sin. God is allowing all these things to happen or not to happen because you are not fully accepted by God even though you still have a chance. It is a dangerous and misleading thesis.

"You can improve your relationship with God by working harder on it"

Since success in life depends on the relationship between you and God, you can do something about it. Repent all your sins. Pray long and well. Fast because some things are not easy, they happen only with fasting and prayer (Mk. 9:29). You can have some exercises and prayer to increase your faith (Lk. 17:9), and the church provides some training sessions and retreats to increase your faith. It is misleading. Many have done these things and their situations did not produce the wished for results.

"Faithful, generous giving to God, automatically brings prosperity"

There is almost a mathematical formula for material success. Just give at least 10% of all your income to God (tithe), and you can go to the bank for your rewards. God has promised. And tithing is definitely the key as promised in Malachi 3:10: "*bring the full tithe into the storehouse, so that there may be food in my house, and thus put me to the test, says the Lord of hosts; see if I will not open the windows of heaven for you, and pour down for you an overflowing blessing.*" And most tragically, you may be doing the mistake of Ananias and Sapphira (Acts 5:1-11) of not giving fully what you are prescribed to give. Using this argument, there is a lot of abuse, particularly because giving to God virtually means giving to this particular pastor or church. While there is no New Testament evidence of tithing as a practice for the church, pastors are very happy to keep this legalistic demand because it makes a lot of economic sense. And of course, even if you do not get the promised rewards, there will be an explanation which ultimately remains that your failure is only your fault – there is something else you missed. While there is nothing wrong about tithing, we need to examine the theology around it in our churches, so that it does not turn into a legalistic prescription for salvation and material success.

"These things are yours to claim"

The prosperity gospel does not always blame people for a lack of faith, but sometimes attributes a continued lack of wealth and health to the ignorance of the promises of God. Jesus became poor so that you become rich (2 Cor 8:9). God has promised that all things in the world belong to the believers. All houses, all cars, all the money belong to God, and God wants to give them to believers. Just as God said to the Jews in the desert, every land the believers set their foot on is theirs already: "And Moses swore on that day, saying, surely the land on which your foot has trodden shall be an inheritance for you and your children forever, because you have wholeheartedly followed the Lord, my God" (Joshua 14:9). They are yours to claim. Just imagine it, wish for it, and you will certainly get it. Of course it is misleading because it is simply not true and does not happen that way in practice, forcing the prophet or preacher to find a reason why the one in need is not receiving.

Conclusion

In conclusion, I would like to argue that prosperity is not fundamentally evil or in any way incorrect. Let us start with prosperity, or wealth. On the one hand, God must have something to do with prosperity. On the other, prosperity is not a sign of virtue and consequential good relationship with God. At the same time, let us look at poverty. On the one hand, poverty and suffering are not intrinsically evil or a sign of bad relationship with God. On the other hand, poverty is not a virtue for which we must strive and see as a sign of being favoured by God. Both poverty and prosperity have many other factors contributing to the situation, including human factors, societal factors, and injustice in the world, pure luck, and opportunities available for an individual or society.

The prosperity gospel and poverty theology ("good news to the poor"), are both problematic when we put emphasis on the role of the spiritual situation of the respective believer. There is no formula through which one can basically manipulate God. "If you do this…God does this!" If you give more God gives you more. If you repent your sins, God blesses you materially. We need to highlight the sovereignty of God at all times, since God remains *"Deus absconditus"*,[7] a hidden God. The little we know is what God has revealed to

---

[7] From Wikipedia, "The hidden God (Latin: Deus *absconditus*) refers to the Christian idea of the fundamental unknowability of the essence of God. The name comes from the Bible, specifically from the book of Isaiah: "Indeed, you are a hidden God, you God of Israel, the Saviour." (45:15). This concept was particularly important for the thinking of Nicholas of Cusa, Blaise Pascal, John Calvin and Martin Luther. Luther unfolded his views on *Deus absconditus* in his Latin work *De servo arbitrio* in 1525. But he had already hinted at this idea in his lectures on the Psalms, and in his lecture on Romans ten

us, and is sufficient for our salvation. But God remains God, complex to understand, and impossible to put on any template.

There is no ground in the Bible or life experience where we can so precisely determine how God acts in different situations. God refuses to be pinned down through our rationality. God must remain God. From the beginning, people have tried to understand God through history, but God does not fit any descriptive formula. The question of why bad things happen to good people and good things to bad people has been there forever. From the time of Moses, to the time of the psalmists in the Proverbs and all wisdom writings; from individual cases like that of Job, to the death of Jesus himself; from lives of people like Paul and other post-New Testament people we know, it has never been possible to fix God in some template. Why evil people succeed materially, and God lets small children in some countries die so early from preventable diseases, are questions every pastor must find a nightmare to answer to Sunday school children or our own children.

History is a witness that despite faith, despite prayer, Christians still get sick, lack food and a good life, die early, experience suffering, fail examinations, get demoted at work, their houses collapse during earthquakes, and their money gets stolen. After praying for so long, singing through the night, refusing to go to hospital to get treatment because of faith, people realize that they shall never be good enough or that what they heard is simply wrong. It is not good news to continue putting so unrealistic and baseless expectations on the believers. Sooner or later, they realize it is not working for them. They should never be given an impression that it is their fault, or they do not believe enough, or that their salvation is not complete. What is proclaimed as the good news of promise, quickly becomes the bad news of rejection and unworthiness before God.

I would also urge us as the church to look at how we identify key tenets or aspects of negative, wrong, misleading prosperity theology. There are too many abuses of this theology which lead to a violation of dignity of the people of God. Among many, Joe Carter mentions some marks of a wrong theology of prosperity as follows, which I find helpful:[8]

> 1. The absence of a serious doctrine of the biblical necessity and normalcy of suffering, the absence of a doctrine of suffering;
> 2. The absence of a clear and prominent doctrine of self-denial is a tip off that something is amiss;
> 3. The absence of a serious exposition of Scripture (*beyond selective proof-texting*);
> 4. The absence of dealing with tensions in Scripture;

---

years earlier. The opposite of *Deus absconditus* in Lutheran theology is *Deus revelatus* (the revealed God), accessed on January 6, 2021

[8] https://www.thegospelcoalition.org/article/what-you-should-know-about-the-prosperity-gospel/

5. Church leaders who have exorbitant lifestyles;
6. A prominence of self and a marginalization of the greatness of God.[9]

Finally, I would like to propose a fresh look at the concept of blessing, or a theology of blessing, as a positive prosperity theology. I think the concept of "blessing" is one possible key to address the complexities in a prosperity gospel. Christians, particularly in Africa, take blessing seriously, and they invite pastors to pronounce a blessing at different occasions in Christians lives: e.g. weddings, ground-breaking for a new house, opening of a new house, and a new car. At a close of any service, all people, poor or rich, wait to receive the Aaronic blessing as proclaimed:

> "The Lord bless you and keep you; the Lord make his face to shine upon you, and be gracious to you, the Lord lift up his countenance upon you, and give you peace" (Num 6:24-26).

Once in my congregation in Germany, a pastor who was fixated at finishing the service within one hour forgot this last blessing and dismissed the congregation. An elderly lady shouted: "Don't we get any blessings today?" The pastor had to swallow his pride and offer the blessing as expected. This is because Christians understand God to be active in their lives, and give testimony to this fact that they have received or experienced God's blessings, sometimes asking congregations to join them in thanksgiving. Some churches have a regular thanksgiving to encourage each and every one to think of something to thank God for, and many do, rich or poor. The main point here is to draw the attention of every member to contemplate the presence of God in their lives.

The concept of blessing could provide a key to correct both the misleading triumphalistic theology of prosperity, as well as the demeaning message which tend to present poverty and suffering as somehow godly or virtuous. We should not demonize success and well-being, or bring guilt feelings to successful people as if all wealth is from evil or is evil by itself. It is indeed a sign of blessing as well. There must be good news also to the wealthy, since they are also under the love of God, and God is happy when people are enjoying life. On the other hand, we must reject the notion that prosperity is a sign of approval of our faith and obedience to God. It is by grace and opportunity. The concept of blessing separates salvation from success completely. Neither the rich nor the poor are justified because of their social situation, but are all covered by the grace of our Lord, through the blood of Christ, and are justified through faith.

---

[9] I once challenged a friend of mine to just not make references to anything he has done or said before in his next sermon, and let him see how much remains. It is normally about the preacher, even more than about God and Christ.

The concept of blessing may also bring good news to those who are materially unsuccessful. Their unwanted situation is not always caused by the rich. It is not always caused by themselves either. The concept provides the key to understand and possibly accept the situations of those with incurable diseases, those who suffer from the effects of natural disasters like earthquakes, floods and droughts, but also to encourage them to look and probably find the presence of God and blessings. Moreover, the fact is that even in the harshest circumstances which refuse to leave, the presence of God and small blessings for which we may be thankful are assured and encouraged. It is like when we sit on a side of a dying patient, knowing our prayers and efforts of all human expertise some time come to an end. But exactly at that time we can hear thankfulness and praise from the mouth of the dying believer, and acknowledgement of the presence of God, who has both the future and the present at hand. There are times to hear what Paul heard after God refused to take away his "thorn in the flesh": *"there was given me a thorn in my flesh, a messenger of Satan, to torment me. Three times I pleaded with the Lord to take it away from me. But he said to me, 'My grace is sufficient for you, for my power is made perfect in weaknesses."* (2Cor 12:7-9)

However, this concept of blessing leaves God to be God as we look at different circumstances of people. God chooses to bless people differently. In the same family, people are born with different capabilities and characters, which at the end make them succeed very differently in life. Some are born with inherited chronic diseases. Some are born in deserts and others in rain forests. Some are born in countries with a developed infrastructure while others must spend hours walking to hospital. Why are some people still basically gatherers and hunters, while others are planning to move to live on other planets? Trying to look for this *"Deus absconditus"* to find an explanation of God doing so, is falling into the trap of the Lutheran understanding of "theology of glory," which is in principle about God's limited self-revelation to humanity. Here I would agree with Luther, that what God has not decided to reveal to us should be left like that.

The concept of blessing is not intended to pacify people here and lead them to resignation caused by a wrong notion of predestination, therefore, not to fight for their rights or work for the betterment of their situation. It is rather to allow the sovereignty of God. For God decides to bless not when we are idle, but during the fulfilment of our responsibilities. It leaves us room to see the importance of human activity in our life, which is susceptible to human sinful nature. It allows us to examine injustice which humans inflict on others, causing the majority of the global problems on other human beings, and to conduct our work of advocacy and working for justice. Many people are in poverty because of oppressive systems, as well as individual and cultural factors such as laziness, dependency syndrome, exploitation by others, conflicts as well as environmental destruction. We should work for peace without which no prosperity is possible. We must fight corruption which deprives people of their chances to progress. We must work to create enabling conditions, so that peoples' gifts can be fairly utilized to improve their lives. We must reject exploitative theologies which give the impression that those who demand us to give to them in order to support their ostentatious living are not God-sent. Likewise, we must reject unreasonable and exploitative demands brought to us in fake and selfish prophesies. We must support those who criticize and prosecute self-proclaimed leaders who manipulate church members by issuing false threats and promises. These kinds of threats and promises aim at taking financial resources from the poor and giving to the rich, by falsely claimed divine authority. Self-proclaimed leaders must be accountable and enforced, if necessary, by national laws.

Trending Facets of Wealth and Prosperity Gospel in Kenya
Joseph Mutei

"The church began as a movement in Jerusalem. It became a philosophy in Greece, an institution in Rome, a culture in Europe, and when it came to America, it became a business...a highly profitable business. But Jesus is coming back for a movement."[1]

The prosperity gospel has been presented in different versions, both the negative as well as the positive. The positive is where it is presented as generosity, charity, philanthropy and benevolence. This is not only welcome but a great way of expressing the Christian faith in the continent.

Yet on the ground, things are different with prosperity theology being used mainly for enriching church leaders through manipulating people with false promises and peddling false hopes.

The Origin and Entry of Prosperity Gospel to Kenya

The prosperity gospel in Kenya came through the preaching of American televangelists and the importation by local preachers visiting various parts of the world. Several factors in the local socio-religious context paved the way for the establishment of the prosperity movement in Kenya. Such factors as the religiosity of Kenyans, poverty levels, and the desire to try some new religious experiences.

In Kenya, the prosperity gospel is largely known as the health and wealth gospel or the gospel of success. The prosperity gospel is a doctrine within the Christian faith which states that financial blessing is the will of God for Christians, and that faith, positive speech and donations to Christian ministries will always increase one's material wealth.[2] O'Donovan[3] refers to prosperity theology as a form of false teaching that has gained a large following in Africa today. This is the teaching that God does not want any of his children to be

---

[1] The Gathering, *The Gospel Enterprise*, San Mateo; 2014. https://thegathering.com/the-gospel-enterprise/ accessed 2nd November 2020.
[2] M.S. Asamoah, 'Penteco/Charismatic Worldview of Prosperity Theology.' *African Educational Research Journal*, v. 1 (3), 2013, pp. 198-208.
[3] Wibur O'Donovan, *Biblical Christianity in Modern Africa: Prosperity Theology*, Carlisle; aternoster Press, 2000.

poor or to lack anything they might desire.[4] The prosperity gospel teaches people to focus on getting, not giving.

That the prosperity gospel has infiltrated the continent of Africa is a statement of fact rather than speculation. From North to South, West to East, the health and wealth gospel preaching the doctrines of financial blessing as being the will of God for all believers, and positive speech and donations to Christian ministries as a means for material increase, is evident across the continent. Originating from the teachings of such prominent preachers in the U.S.A. as Kenneth Hagin and Kenneth Copeland, the movement has over the years metamorphosed into different shapes and sizes when domesticated in the different parts of the African soil.

Inaccurate Exegesis and Hermeneutics

Proponents of the prosperity gospel in Kenya are fond of flashing some well-choreographed and memorised texts to their audience. There are many but only to list a few:
- Deuteronomy 8:18 – But remember the LORD your God, for it is he who gives you the ability to produce wealth, and so confirms his covenant, which he swore to your forefathers, as it is today.
- Malachi 3:10 – Bring the whole tithe into the storehouse, that there may be food in my house. Test me in this, says the LORD Almighty, and see if I will not throw open the floodgates of heaven and pour out so much blessing, that you will not have room enough for it.
- Luke 6:38 – Give, and it will be given to you. A good measure, pressed down, shaken together and running over, will be poured into your lap. For with the measure you use, it will be measured to you. (This verse is quoted to encourage members to give.)
- John 10:10 – The thief comes only to steal and kill and destroy; I have come that they may have life, and have it to the full. (However, is this about physical well-being or different?)
- 3 John 2 – Dear friend, I pray that you may enjoy good health and that all may go well with you, even as your soul is getting along well. (This has been seen as the ultimate goal of life here on earth. That is to live large, enjoy life and almost end it all here.)

Citation out of Context

One of the first slogans you learn in a seminary is "Context is king." It is impossible to grasp the true meaning of a statement without knowing the

---

[4] C. Mwikamba, C. & S. Ifedha, 'Blessed Are the Rich and Prosperous For Theirs Is the Kingdom of the World: The Kenyan Challenge,' *Research on Humanities and Social Sciences,* v.5, No.14, 2015.

context. Without the literary context, there is no meaning at all; all we have are possible meanings. Often, due to lack of context, prosperity preachers end up with Eisogesis, that is, reading into the text. This is the corrupting gift all prosperity preachers share. Here are a few common examples:

- You do not have because you do not ask (James 4:2b). Prosperity preachers use this verse to teach their followers to "name it and claim it." When you read this verse properly in context, you realize that James is not primarily instructing us how to pray, but condemning our covetousness (James 4:1–4).
- Do not be deceived: God is not mocked, for whatever one sows, that will he also reap (Galatians 6:7). Prosperity preachers use this verse to promise their followers greater rewards if they give greater amounts of money to the preacher. The next verses in context explain that the sowing is "doing good", and what we reap for doing good is "eternal life" (Galatians 6:8–9). The verse has nothing to do with money.
- Christ redeemed us ... so that in Christ Jesus the blessing of Abraham might come to the Gentiles (Galatians 3:13a, 14a). Prosperity preachers use this verse to teach that God will give us the material blessings he promised to Abraham. If you read the entire verse, however, you find that Paul explains what he means by the blessing of Abraham. It is "the promised Spirit" (Galatians 3:14b).
- Though he was rich, yet for your sake he became poor, so that you, by his poverty, might become rich (2 Corinthians 8:9). Obviously, prosperity preachers interpret this verse to be about money. But what does Paul mean? Just a few verses before, he talks about the Macedonian churches being in "extreme poverty." They are not rich, but Paul says they have a "wealth of generosity" (2 Corinthians 8:2).

These kind of examples could go on and on because prosperity preachers always ignore the context of what they are preaching. I once attended a prosperity church and listened to a sermon entitled "Your Lost Glory." The prophetess preached from Luke 15:8, which says, "Or what woman, having ten silver coins, if she loses one coin, does not light a lamp and sweep the house and seek diligently until she finds it?" To my dismay, she came on stage with a broom and said we needed to sweep our spiritual houses and find our lost glory. She named the lost glory of marriage, education, and visas. Although I was shocked by such a misreading of God's word, I was far more surprised by the excitement in the crowd and the number of people falling down under her "anointing." If you read the context of this verse, you find that Jesus is giving a parable to describe heaven's joy "over one sinner who repents" (Luke 15:10). Sadly, the preaching that evening did not produce any heavenly joy. No one was urged to repent; they were taught only to covet.

One easy way to protect yourself and others from false teaching is to read the literary context. That is all. Read the whole chapter of Luke. Read the whole book of Luke. Know what the author is trying to communicate so that you will not be so easily deceived.

Too Literal

Another misleading method of interpretation in the prosperity gospel movement is reading figurative language in scripture as literal. You often hear followers say, for example, "Jesus died so we can live abundant lives." Jesus did say, *"I came so that they may have life and have it in abundance"* (John 10:10). In context, though, Jesus is contrasting himself with false teachers who are like a thief who "comes only to steal and to kill and destroy." If we take this literally, Jesus is saying that, instead of taking from our homes and treasuries, he will fill them with abundance. However, should we read this verse literally? Is it possible Jesus is using figurative language to communicate spiritual truth?

When we think of the context, we not only think of the verses surrounding the verse but also the whole book. How does John use the word *life* throughout the entire gospel? *Life* in the book of John almost always refers to eternal life. So we must consider the possibility that the life Jesus is describing is not present but future. In John 10:10, "abundant life" is rich imagery for the eternal life of the Kingdom, as depicted in other portions of scripture (cf.Isaiah 35:1–10; 55:12–13; 65:17–25; Micah 4:1–5; Zechariah 14:1–21). Bruce Milne notes that this abundant life "is glimpsed briefly in Eden, and seen in vision in Revelation as a city coming down from God, the holy dwelling of God with his people. It is the life for which we were created.[5]

The Future Now

Book titles like *Your Best Life Now*[6] which sell millions of copies worldwide, reveal another major misinterpretation. Prosperity preachers ignore the concept of the "already but not yet." For them, there are no future promises. The kingdom of heaven has already come in its fullness. So, we can have perfect health now. We can enjoy suffering-free lives now. Some prosperity preachers even teach that we will not die if we have faith. "Death is not your portion," they declare. It is very awkward when these preachers die.

In the Old Testament, the prophets predicted the fulfilment of many great promises at the coming of Christ. In the New Testament, we discover that some of these promises are fulfilled at Jesus's first coming, while others will be fulfilled when he comes again. Prosperity preachers' failure to grasp this concept leads to drawing too much of the future into the present.

---

[5] https://www.desiringgod.org/articles/the-gods-of-the-prosperity-gospel#fn11
[6] https://www.desiringgod.org/articles/the-gods-of-the-prosperity-gospel#fn12

Misapplication

After we interpret the meaning of a scriptural text, we should apply it to our lives. If a prosperity preacher makes a baby step toward proper interpretation of a text's meaning, he will likely fail woefully in the application of it, a failure that says he never really properly interpreted. A prime example is the application of the phrase *"Touch not my anointed"* (1 Chronicles 16:22; Psalm 105:15).[7] Prosperity preachers teach that you cannot criticize or speak against them, the "men of God," because God says, *"Touch not my anointed."* That is their application of the text, and that is how they elevate themselves. This is one way the "man of God" becomes more important than Christ himself. This is how they even escape jail. A Nigerian prosperity preacher recently confessed to his congregation that he committed adultery because his wife did the same. But there were no ecclesiastical or legal consequences because church members fear touching the *"anointed man of God."*[8] In these churches, it is more tolerable to speak blasphemously about Christ than to speak a word against the man of God because the anointed supposedly cannot and should never be questioned or touched, and followers never question their teaching.

These errors are being actively transferred from one corner of the world to the other, and they are spreading like wild fire. The direction that should be taken is that of Christ-centred biblical theology. In this endeavour, fidelity would be given to proper exegesis as well as faithful adherence to hermeneutical procedures. These will mitigate against the carefree and loose interpretations for an immediate gratification of the prosperity preachers.

Pillars of the Prosperity Gospel in Kenya

The tenets of health and wealth prosperity teaching are the following:

1. Faith

Like many other prosperity thinkers, faith is seen more as positive thinking. Members are encouraged to think positively as a way of exercising faith. This leads to the kind of faith whereby it is seen as a way of getting things from God.

2. Positive confession

The positive confession has to do with the power of the spoken word. What you say, you cause God to 'deliver'. This, coupled with the positive thinking, makes the followers feel empowered to think themselves into possessing anything and everything they desire in the name of 'faith'.

---

[7] https://www.desiringgod.org/articles/the-gods-of-the-prosperity-gospel#fn13
[8] https://www.desiringgod.org/articles/the-gods-of-the-prosperity-gospel#fn14

3. The seed faith principle

The principle teaches that church members are to bring their money, seeds, poultry, or even cows, to the man or woman of God to be prayed over for multiplication. It assumes that what one gives to God must always multiply and that 'Those that sow big will reap big'. Unfortunately, in Kenya, this has led to the enriching of the pastors while impoverishing the congregants.

4. Urban-Based Congregations

The prosperity gospel churches mostly target the professionals and middle working classes with economic powers within the urban centres. The churches are set up in classy ways, making them very attractive but with the intention of attracting the resourced members, who in turn are called upon to give in order to receive their blessings speedily.

5. Good Networking, Mentorship and Intimacy

The well-established prosperity gospel churches are good at building networks and mentorships. Seminary training is one of the chief means of building their networks. A good number of the rich prosperity gospel preachers have their own theological college and seminary. They also connect well with all who attend church services through phone calls, emails, newsletters and the social media.

6. Effective Media and Publications

Prosperity gospel preachers use media and publications pitched at a very high visual level to attract many to themselves. Today, many of the prosperity preachers have their own media houses, websites, tv and radio stations, and a variety of publications professionally presented to sell the church activities.

Manifestation of Prosperity Gospel in Kenya

Prosperity Gospel is manifest in Kenya through some key proponents of its teachings.

1. Pastor Victor Kanyari

He is well known in the media circles for his 'fake' cures/miracles that caught media attention in the recent past. Pastor Victor Kanyari would ask gullible people of faith to "plant seeds" by contributing about Ksh. 310 to his "ministry" in exchange for immediate miraculous answers to their prayers.

2. Bishop Margaret Wanjiru

The flamboyant bishop is the founder of Jesus is Alive Ministries and immediate former assistant Minister and Starehe Member of Parliament (MP). She lives big, and preaches about her followers making it big in life through accessing 'the glory'. Her slogan of 'the glory is here' is used to draw people to her church as the place to access their economic and spiritual breakthroughs.

3. Bishop Allan and Rev. Cathy Kiuna

Bishop Allan and Rev Kathy Kiuna are in a league of their own in the church circles. The flamboyant couple has a mega-church in the Ngara area of Nairobi city known as the Jubilee Christian Centre. Through the church members' contribution, the couple live big with a palatial home in Runda, which is an upmarket area of Nairobi, Kenya. Their teaching, especially targeting young professionals, has seen the tapping of a lot of monetary resources from the working class. The teachings are geared towards promising quick prosperity to those who 'stand' with the work of God through their ministry. During such things as their birthdays, members are asked to offer 'big' gifts including such cars as BMWs and Range Rover Sports, and these are not cheap both to buy and to maintain. Their response to their critiques who see no reason as to why they should exploit their congregation in this way is by saying: "God wants us to be prosperous in every single way. His desire for us is to walk in abundance. We are praying for church people to show the likes of Bill Gates dust." This is interpreted to mean that the two should be raised to the level of Bill Gates and beyond through the monetary support received through their church members.

4. Prophet Dr. David Owuor

Prophet Dr. David Owuor is a prosperity preacher based in Nakuru, Kenya, but with churches spread across the country. Apart from his controversial sources of wealth, his teachings and practices have attracted a lot of criticism. The self-proclaimed prophet allegedly never collects offerings in his ministries, begging the question of how he makes his money. For instance, Prophet Owuor has made claims that are against the mainstream orthodox Christian doctrines. These claims include: a) anyone needing to see the Father must go through him, and b), he has access to heaven where he visits frequently, among others. In terms of his practices, Prophet Owuor moves around in a presidential-style convoy comprising sleek black Mercedes cars, accompanied by siren blaring police outriders taking the lead, clearing the way. Prophet Owuor's Ministry of Repentance and Holiness Church has very strict rules for the followers with no room for contravening them, lest you are punished.

5. Thomas Wahome, Brother Paul Kamlesh Pattni and Apostle James Maina Ng'ang'a

These prosperity gospel preachers have courted different controversies, with some exhibiting non-orthodox ways to attract members into their mega-churches. These churches are 'personal', and those who deviate from their teachings are reprimanded or expelled from the churches with very little recourse.

Conclusion

The Bible is the central book guiding the life and practice of Christians. The pivotal place held by the Bible has seen many guided and nourished by its teachings with immediate and eternal hopes. The key to receiving this spiritual nourishment and guidance on things of the world lies in the understanding of the messages therein, and the application of the same to the believer's context. Through such disciplines as exegesis, hermeneutics and application, the fidelity of the word and the sanctity of the message is assured.

Nevertheless, the prosperity preachers do not take this path to unearth the gospel truth and, therefore, appropriate it for the good of the church in the contemporary context. Instead they use non-orthodox means in reaching to conclusions from the scriptures that best fit to serve their interests by hoodwinking their followers to believe that their interpretation of scriptures is the best for their health, wealth and prosperity.

If the Kenyan church is going to overcome these upcoming teachings, there is need to go back to the drawing board and ensure that preachers are well trained theologically in order for them to 'truthfully teach the Word of God'.[9] There is need for regulating the starting of churches with clear affiliation of pastors and denominations with national and regional councils which will oversee their activities and play the advisory role, keeping them to observe the correct teachings. Finally, there is need to offer regular refresher training on pastoral ethics. These will help in safeguarding against malpractices that are being witnessed currently, where slowly the church is losing out on its prophetic role to the society due to some of the unethical practices being witnessed within her ranks. Above all, we need to pray that the Lord will continue 'building His church', which the gates of Hades cannot overcome.[10]

---

[9] 2 Timothy 2:15.
[10] Matthew 16:18.

Theological Impact of Wealth and Prosperity Gospel in Tanzania
Mary L. Kategile

There are many definitions of prosperity, According to the Advanced Learner's Dictionary of Current English, prosperity is the state of being "successful, and having good fortune". Furthermore, Ayantayo,[1] defined prosperity gospel as a strong teaching that requires Christians to be prosperous while on earth. He says prosperity theology teaches that God wants his people to be prosperous and healthy in life, with wealth being used as the measure for one's level of favour with God. In addition, according to van Biema and Chu,[2] the prosperity gospel is the doctrine that God wants people to be prosperous, especially financially. The world mission conference that was held in Lausanne in 2010 stated that "Prosperity gospel is the teaching that believers have a right to the blessings of health and wealth and that they can obtain these blessings through positive confessions of faith and the 'sowing of seeds' through the faithful payments of tithes and offerings".[3]

From the definitions above one can realize that wealth and prosperity gospel preaching is about calling people to be prosperous in wealth and health while you are in this world. Horton[4] argues that the prosperity gospel is the modern gospel that is marketed to consumers and not proclaimed to penitent sinners. Concurrent with Horton's argument is Stott's[5] observation that the movement preaches that God has empowered them to help believers get out of their liability and meet their financial needs. It is proclaimed that it is the will of God that people should prosper so they can give abundantly in spreading the gospel. The theology of the prosperity gospel has been complex in many ways, and the complexities have caused it to be recognized as a misleading theology.

---

[1] J.K. Ayantayo, "*Prosperity Gospel and Social Morality: A Critique.* In David Ogungbile and Akintunde Akinade (eds.) *Creativity and Change in Nigeria Christianity.* Lagos: Malthouse Press, 2017, p. 203.
[2] David van Biema, and Jeff Chu, "Does God Want You to Be Rich?" *Time*, September 18, 2006, pp. 48-56.
[3] Lausanne Theology Working Group Statement on the Prosperity Gospel,' *Evangelical Review of Theology,* 34.3 (2010), pp. 99-102, 99.
[4] M. Horton, *The agony of deceit.* Chicago, Ill: Moody Press, 1990, p. 28.
[5] J. Stott, *Understanding the Bible.* Grand Rapids, MI: Baker Books, 1984, pp. 226-227.

Intricacies of Preaching Wealth and Prosperity Gospel in Tanzania

The society that we live in is thirsty for the word of God. There is a quest for a better life, and poverty is making people wish to become rich in easy ways. But also people want miracles, hence the desire for shortcuts to solve their problems. This became obvious for many who recall a few years ago that a retired Lutheran pastor came up with an idea that he had received a revelation from God to prepare the medicine that will heal people from different infirmities at Samunge Loliondo, Tanzania. Thousands of Tanzanians went to Arusha for that cup, famously called *'Kikombe cha Babu'* (a grandfather's cup). As Makulilo describes:

> In 2011, tens of thousands of people from all over East Africa flocked to Loliondo in Tanzania seeking a cure for several diseases, including diabetes, tuberculosis and HIV. Ambilikile Mwasapile, a former Lutheran pastor, administered a miracle dose popularly known as "*kikombe*", charging about $0.33 for his concoction per patient. The Ministry of Health while concluding that the dose in Babu's "cup" was safe, did not endorse such drink as a "cure".[6]

The result was that many people who drunk the cup were not healed but he made a fortune. This shows that people are suffering physically as well as spiritually and are desperate to find quick and simple solutions. Early in year 2020, it was announced that more than twenty people died in Moshi, Tanzania, after stamping on each other on their way to stamp on the oil that was spread on a carpet or mat by a preacher who calls himself Bulldozer. The preacher uses the so-called anointed oil, which he claims has the power to heal and cleanse all bad spirits that one had stepped on or been bewitched by. In an interview with Abagile,[7] who attended the worship at that church, he explained that people are suffering from being bewitched and some other diseases, hence they need to be cleansed by the anointed oil. The instruction goes that after you step on the oil, then you have to buy the holy water which by drinking continues to sanctify you. He further said that there is usually a call for those who want to send the gospel by their offerings; the preacher prays for them according to an amount they are willing to give. There were those who gave Tsh 100,000/=, 50,000/=, 20,000/= and 10,000/=. Prayers depend on how much you are going to give, and it will determine the amount of blessings one will receive. This kind of preaching is misleading because it influences people to believe in things and the preacher, rather than believing in the power of God in Jesus Christ.

---

[6] Alexander Makulilo, Alexander, "'You must only drink one cup": Revisiting the tension between "Kikombe cha Babu" and biomedicine in Tanzania.' In *The African Review*, vol. 45, Number 2, 2018, p. 32.
[7] Interview with Abagile, Kalundo 17 November 2020, Mbeya.

Goliama contends that the "prosperity theology insists that the root cause of poverty is bondage with the past traditional African culture".[8] This means bondage with village culture, ancestral veneration, the extended family system, and the culture of commensality in general, while, according to Martin, "African culture embodies the spirit of poverty, since it is associated with witchcraft and backwardness".[9] Several church leaders, pastors, and some self-proclaimed prophets and apostles in Tanzania give themselves titles such as Anointed Elder (Mzee wa Upako), Bulldozer, and Devil's Whipper (Kiboko ya shetani).

Misinterpretation of the Gospel

The prosperity theology is misleading since it distorts the meaning and interpretation of scriptures. Some of the mostly used scriptures are: *'But you are a chosen people, a royal priesthood, a holy nation, God's special possession, that you may declare the praises of Him who called you out of darkness into His wonderful light'* (1 Peter 2:9). Such verses are interpreted to convince the listener that what it says points to you directly right now in this life. Thus the preaching goes that you cannot be of royal priesthood without being rich and prosperous. You cannot declare the praises of God if you are poor hence the servant of God has been sent to make you rich and acquire more wealth. Furthermore, Proverbs 3:9-10 ESV: *Honour the Lord with your wealth and with the first fruits of all your produce; then your barns will be filled with plenty, and your vats will be bursting with wine.* This text encourages members to give more as the way of honouring God. Indeed, it is important honour God with our offering, but the problem comes when only the barns of preachers are filled, and not those of members. These kind of teachings are carried out by many prosperity gospel's adherents hence they attract many people.

The gospel focuses primarily on material possessions, physical well-being, and success in this life, which includes abundant financial resources, good health, clothes, housing, cars, promotion at work, and success in business. This gospel asserts that believers have the right to the blessings of health and wealth, and that they can obtain these blessings through positive confessions of faith, and the 'sowing of seeds' through the faithful payments of tithes and offerings. The extent of material acquisition and well-being is often equated with God's approval. Although the Bible affirms that God cares enough to bless his people and provide for their needs, and although there are legitimate ways to work for such needs to be met, this gospel often makes the pursuit of material things and physical well-being ends in themselves. Scripture is always applied and

---

[8] Castor Michael Goliama, 'The Gospel of Prosperity in African Pentecostalism: A Theological and Pastoral Challenge to the Catholic Church – with Reference to the Archdiocese of Songea, Tanzania.' Ph.D. Thesis, 2013.
[9] D. Martin, *Pentecostalism: The World Their Parish.* Oxford: Blackwell, 2002, p. 26.

sometimes misinterpreted or manipulated to promote the main emphasis of the prosperity gospel.

Paul writes, "Whatsoever a man sows sparingly, will also reap sparingly, and whoever sows generously will also reap generously (1Corinthians 9:6). You give as seed; you receive it back multiplied many times." This is contrary to what true teaching of the Gospel stipulates in Luke 6:38: *Give and it will be given to you: good measure, pressed down, shaken together, and running over will be put into your bosom. For with the same measure that you use, it will be measured back to you.'* This verse is often quoted, followed by a sermon which emphasises the benefits of giving. This is the most popular verse used in appealing to the congregation to give in order to finance projects of the church. This is not only to the adherents of prosperity gospel but even to those in mainline churches. The text is neither about giving to God financially, nor expecting returns for what we give. It has to do with loving and forgiving one another, as well as being of service without expecting anything in return. In most cases, members are made to be anxious to receive returns for their giving here and now. Then when they do not receive, some go astray and go to other churches in search of a better life, hence they end up doing denominational window-shopping. This has, however, been twisted to indicate that God will return in double or hundred-fold whatever one gives in offerings. It is common for several collections to be taken in a single service. For many denominations, one can find that in one service, there are four or even more offerings with the emphasis on giving in anticipation of God's reward with material blessings. Positive confession is encouraged for good health, wealth and other blessings.

Preaching as Employment

Many preachers of the prosperity gospel in Tanzania have introduced different kinds of offerings with the intention of collecting more money from members, and those who attend their churches in need of prayers. These offerings include planting the seeds and offering for whatever need that you have. The teaching of planting of the seeds offering encourages people to give with the expectation of getting more from God. Some people fall into heavy debt as they would be lured to sell their properties for the sake of "planting a seed" so as to harvest money in return. When things do happen contrary to the fake promises of the preachers, the faithful retreat as far as they can, and think that all preachers are made to exploit them rather than showing them the love of Christ amidst life's challenges be they economic, spiritual, or health. Another offering is called *'Jimalize',* meaning empty yourself then God will fill your pockets. The preacher gave a call that people should give all the money they have in their pockets and wallets, then he will pray that God will provide all their needs. This kind of offering has been painful to many, since after giving they do not see their pockets being filled.

There is one preacher in Mbeya who calls himself a prophet. He has gained popularity in this city for the last five years. At his church, he sells oil, salt and stones. These things are sold to people who go there for worship and other different life problems. In an interview with a 58 years-old woman by the name of Sophia who attended worship service at that church when she was caring for a sick sister, she explained:

> I took my sister there for healing prayers; she had suffered for more than one year. When we reached there and the time for us to see the prophet came he explained that he has power for healing which he was given by God, and that he had the ability to go to hell to redeem those who died through witchcraft. He prayed for her, and then he told us that we need to give offering and then buy the things he was selling. The oil was for anointing, the salt was to keep the witches away, and that the stones he will give only to those people who wanted to join that church as full-time members. He then explained that the stones are given in reference to the stone that David used to kill Goliath (1 Samuel 17:49).[10]

From that interview it was discovered that the preacher's main aim is material gain from his members. Generally, preachers who focus on material gain are mostly concentrated in urban areas where Christians are in large numbers and most of them are economically well-off compared to the majority of those in rural areas. Those living in urban areas struggle to earn a living. Thus, they are easily trapped by the cheap preaching that requires them to give offerings and get back wealth through prayers.

Controversy on Understanding Living for the Gospel and Living out of the Gospel

The perspective of living for the gospel is based on the core calling to preach the gospel. When Jesus was calling his first disciples in Matthew 4: 18 and Mark 1:16, he said, 'Follow me'. Peter and Andrea did not hesitate to leave everything and follow Jesus. That is to say, they left the profession to which they were making a living and followed Jesus. Jesus sending his disciples directly applies to the sending out of the prosperity gospel preachers today. According to the great commission in Matthew 28: 18-20: *All authority in heaven and on earth has been given to me! Therefore go and make disciples of all nations, baptizing them in the name of the Father and of the Son and of the Holy Spirit, and teaching them to obey everything I have commanded you. And surely I am with you always, to the very end of the age.* In the great commission, we have a command to go, that is, going without expecting anything in return from the people you are going to preach to.

---

[10] Interview with Sophia Kanema, 14 November 2020, Mbeya.

Many adherents of prosperity gospel live out of the gospel as contrary to living for the gospel. Living out of the gospel means they preach so that they can gain materially and fame. Hence, they make sure that they earn as much as they can out of the gospel. As the emphasis is strongly placed on material acquisition, which could be manifested in the possession of cars, houses, bank accounts, cash at hand, clothing, abundance, fortune and success in all endeavours, which make prosperity, Christians must seek divine favour and pursue it with vigour. Lindhardt asserts: "a central insight of sociological theories of religious markets or religious economies is that competition in unregulated markets tends to produce the kind of religious products that consumers prefer and demand".[11] It follows that religious consumption is higher in a market situation where plurality and freedom of choice prevail.

Advocates of the prosperity gospel believe that wealth is a sign of God's blessing and the poor are poor because of a lack of faith. In an interview with sixty years-old Loyce,[12] when she was asked to give her opinion on the prosperity gospel that is being preached in her local church she said that the problem with some preachers is that they turned it into a money-making venture, and diverted from the biblical principles concerning wealth. This statement goes in line with a Ghanaian woman, who said:

> All I see are pastors, reverends, bishops and the like getting richer and richer, whilst their congregation looks on, praying and hoping that one day; they will also be as wealthy as the pastor. Can't these people open their eyes and see it is their monies enriching these so-called pastors? Djanie.[13]

Intricacy of Wealth and Prosperity Gospel in Tanzania

In Tanzania, there is an ever growing number of preachers, self-proclaimed anointed prophets and apostles. These have gained popularity based on their spiritual and material wealth. Many of these preachers exhibit extraordinary riches which they accumulate from the offerings of many poor people. The emphases of preaching have been on how to acquire wealth and prosper in life. Suffice it to point out that this teaching counts material blessings as a sign of God's favour on a believer. Many Tanzanian Christians living in the context of grinding poverty find a compelling reason to join the churches that preach this doctrine in the hope of alleviating their plight.

Adherents of the prosperity gospel believe that wealth is a sign of God's blessing, and is compensation for prayer and for giving beyond the minimum

---

[11] M. Lindhardt, 'Miracle Makers and Money Takers: Healers, Prosperity Preachers and Fraud in Contemporary Tanzania.' In Amanda van Eck (ed.) *In Good Faith: Minority Religions and Fraud.* Aldershot: Ashgate, 2012. pp. 153–180.
[12] Interview with Loyce Ludisha, on 23/10/2020.
[13] A. Djanie, 'Losing my Soul.' In *New African*, No. 503, February 2011, p. 35.

tithe to one's church or other religious causes. The logical extension of the prosperity gospel is sometimes explicit and sometimes not. This depends on the preachers who claim that the poor are poor because of a lack of faith, and that poverty is the fault of the poor themselves. Obviously when it comes to the matters of faith, even intelligent people can believe anything, as long as they have been influenced by another person who claims to have the power of God almighty.

Human beings can believe anything that seems to be beyond ones understanding. This has led many to follow and believe different preachers in hope of solving their problems. Goliama says:

> The root causes of poverty common to Tanzania as a whole are widely perceived to be the following: the aftermath of the *Ujamaa* political ideology, neo-liberal policies and Structural Adjustment Programmes, the spread of HIV/AIDS pandemic, corruption, exploitation of the land's resources by global companies, and environmental degradation.[14]

That is to say, poverty contributes to people to be attracted to the prosperity gospel with the aim of gaining wealth, and they are willing to give as much as they can as long as they are promised material gain in return. Because the evangelical community of believers acknowledge and accept the scripture as God's authority, we are also bound to live by its instruction.

The promises that are given by the prosperity gospel preachers include God had a purpose in creating you. The ultimate objective of this goal is to make you walk on the hills here on earth to make you an outstanding success. Successful means stand out, be distinguished among others. It is God's will that makes you prosper as long as you give accordingly. Exercise your faith to succeed, and it will lead you through the obstacles to your palace. The prosperity gospel is misleading because it offers an unbalanced application of scripture, which results in a departure from a clear biblical orientation for articulating the doctrine of Jesus Christ. Hence, the ramifications of the prosperity messages, and when measured by fundamental Christological truths, the prosperity gospel becomes a heresy.

In most of the African countries, Neo-Pentecostal and Charismatic churches preach the prosperity gospel by encouraging their members to seek abundant wealth. However, according to Gifford, "it may also apply to the widespread belief in the influence of spirits, for example, if an individual believes an evil spirit is prohibiting financial success, releasing of that evil spirit may provide that individual with energy, helping him or her succeed".[15] It is precisely the relation of the prosperity gospel to scenarios of social change in Africa which

---

[14] C. M. Goliama, 2013, p. 86.
[15] Paul Gifford, *Ghana's new Christianity: Pentecostalism in a globalizing African economy.* Bloomington, IN: Indiana University Press, 2004.

has attracted significant interdisciplinary attention. The prosperity gospel has made steep inroads in academic discourse. In systematic terms, the prosperity gospel deploys a contracted bond of faith, which Kenneth Hagin referred to as the 'law of faith' as quoted by Bowler.[16] As one of the key terms in prosperity theology, the 'law of faith' involves a cause and effect relationship between a believer and God.

Neo-Pentecostal and Charismatic churches in Africa have adopted a business management oriented model in their churches. This model is geared to an aspiration to transform society as well as the socio-economic levels of their members. This is achieved by adopting a sacred secrecy of the prosperity gospel. In the case of contemporary Tanzania, such a clear pattern cannot be found. As in other African countries, many people see both wealth and political power as possible indications of a person's potent alliances with the spiritual world. Insofar as consumers seek spiritual assistance in economic affairs, it seems both logical and reassuring that providers appear to be living proofs of the efficiency of their services. But when traditional healing or the running of a Pentecostal and Charismatic churches in too obvious ways becomes a business venture, and when adherents or consumers fail to see the material fruits of spiritual assistance, doubt can easily be shed on the honesty of those providers.

The theology is called misleading when it lacks a strong theological foundation, and sets aside the mystery of the cross of Jesus Christ. Thus, they reject the invitation of Christ to those who love Him to take His cross and follow Him (Matthew 10:38, 16:24), the profession of faith of the Apostle Paul to which the cross of Christ is the only source of pride (Galatians 6:14). The sermons of prosperity gospel churches follow this pattern: the predestination of members of their cults to reign (political and social power), prosperity (economic power), and the overcoming of disease and occult forces (mystical power). Robbins[17] argued that the explosion of the prosperity gospel in Africa is as a result of a combination of two factors: the first is Pentecostalism which taps into African religio-cultural conditions; the second is the promise of material abundance which exploits the African socio-economic conditions.

The attractiveness of Pentecostalism is also ascribed to what some scholars described as the 'paradox of continuity and rupture', which occurs when Pentecostalism enters a given cultural context. Robbins stated that "in the context of African societies, many women are said to resort to Pentecostalism as a way of escaping from subjugate positions to which they are relegated in the traditionally gendered roles".[18] Indeed, women find Pentecostalism extremely appealing, since it appears to offer them a chance to be recognized,

---

[16] K. Bowler, *Blessed: A history of the American prosperity gospel.* Oxford: Oxford University Press, 2013, pp.44 – 46.
[17] J. Robbins, 'The Globalization of Pentecostal and Charismatic Christianity.' In *Annual Review of Anthropology*, 33, 2004, pp.,121.
[18] Ibid., pp. 121.

and sometimes to have autonomy within such traditionally gendered roles. In church history, we see that women were the first evangelists and were good recipients of the gospel in many places. This has been the case with the preaching of the wealth and prosperity gospel. However, some women have found themselves victims of the prosperity gospel. In Tanzania, many women have been abused by these preachers, and some have gone into bankruptcy and do not know where to go. A woman shared her story with me. A few months after retiring, she was asked by a preacher to take her pension to him so that he can pray and the money would multiply. After doing this, the money never came back and hence she is suffering with high blood pressure. Furthermore, even in some mainline churches women are still excluded in church leadership and ministry. This is also misleading because Jesus never intended the situation to be so.

Aylward and Njiru asserted that "the proponents of the prosperity gospel have often claimed that this teaching embodies a great potential for poverty alleviation. Consequently, many Christians seem to embrace it with the hope of overcoming their poverty and achieving economic advancement through it".[19] However, this has not been the case because it is generally perceived that the greatest beneficiaries of the prosperity gospel are ultimately the preachers. This is clear, since these preachers are becoming richer every day, hence they live luxurious lives, and many of them even have bodyguards.

Many believe that the unfulfilled promise of material prosperity was due to spiritual factors of the lack of faith, and the sin of the individual Christian concerned. It was interesting then to know what the Christians usually do after realizing that the prosperity gospel did not bring forth the expected material blessings. What happens is they leave the church and go to another one. This makes preachers to be like business vendors but in this case the products are prayers and empty promises. Lindhardt says "religious market theories not only focus attention on religious consumers, but also considers the creative advertising of religious institutions and individual entrepreneurs who aspire to generate visibility for themselves and their products".[20] What has been experienced in Tanzania regarding the prosperity gospel and the intricacy of wealth advocacy shows the religious markets theory at work. This causes preachers to use different techniques in making sure that the people listening to preaching are convinced to believe and give generously. Techniques can include lying or even acting, so as to show miracles.

The prosperity gospel has not left the mainline churches safe either because even in our churches it is obvious that the preaching has changed. We hear and see the emphasis on offerings and the planting of seeds. The question for all of us is how will we escape this wave of the prosperity gospel? That is for all of

---

[19] S. Aylward, and J. N. Njiru, *New Religious Movements in Africa.* Nairobi: Pauline Publications Africa, 2001, p. 46.
[20] Lindhardt, 2012.

us to ponder. In our churches, we hear emphasis on giving, more than the sacrament of the Word.

Conclusion

The exhortation from the writer of Hebrews guides us on "fixing our eyes on Jesus, the pioneer and perfecter of our faith. For the joy set before Him, He endured the cross, scorning its shame, and sat down at the right hand of the throne of God" (Hebrews 12:2). We should adhere to this verse in all our ministries.

Packer argued that the Christian principle of biblical authority means on one hand, that God purposes to direct the belief and behaviour of His people through the revealed truth set forth in Holy Scripture; on the other hand, it means that all our ideas about God and life should be measured, tested, and where necessary, corrected and enlarged by reference to biblical teaching.[21] I am in concurrence with Packer's statement for those of us who are here we are called to provide guidelines to sound doctrine based on the Word of God. Sound doctrines can be achieved through theological training to pastors, Christian educators, evangelists, young people, our children and all our members to whom we have been entrusted by God.

---

[21] James I. Packer, *Knowing God: With Study Guide*. London: Hodder & Stoughton, 1993, p. 16.

Prosperity Gospel and its Effects on the Youth in Ethiopia
Tsegahun Assefa Adugna

Beside unemployment, ethnic identity and some other youth related challenges, the prosperity gospel is adding another yoke on the youth in Ethiopia. The prosperity gospel or theology has become a fuel for the youth to expect special blessings from the Lord without hard work. Even for some youths who are working hard for their livelihood, it has created thinking that the Lord is not blessing their work because of their 'immaturity' in faith. Moreover, the biblical interpretation that the propagators of the prosperity gospel are using is far from the historical, literary and grammatical context of the Bible, that the youths are now treating every part of the scripture as pointing towards wealth and health. For the Ethiopian Evangelical Church Mekane Yesus which is a Lutheran church and strictly follows the liturgy and hymn of the early church, the worship programmes are considered as boring for the youth, and a copy of a Western church. The daily assigned Bible readings that the church has been practising are taken as against taking 'fresh' messages from God that will descend at a particular moment as proclaimed by the prosperity gospel preachers. On their television channels the prosperity gospel preachers propagate their healing power and miracles which look like the witchcraft of African Traditional Religions. All these unbiblical practices are leading the youth away from the authentic teaching and spiritual experiences. After losing their resources for nothing, some youths come to realize the truth about the prosperity gospel. Instead of returning to their former churches, these youths tend to close their doors to Christianity or any church related activities and start to question the existence of God. Unless the church gives special attention to equipping youth ministers, it will lose many members who might even go away from orthodox Christianity.

Background of Ethiopian Evangelical Church Mekane Yesus
Ethiopia was a leading country in welcoming Christianity during the time of the apostles, but it existed for more than three hundred years before becoming a state religion. Later, a shift from the gospel to tradition was injected and people started to miss the core meaning of the gospel. This led some international mission agencies, like Hermnasburg Mission, to send missionaries that could

revive Christianity in the country.[1] When this was not successful, a plan to establish a new church was mooted but the challenge from the emperors and the other religions in the country hampered the process. The mission agencies received the green light by the end of the 19th century and their work started to bear fruit.[2] The student and youth movements, together with the Pentecostal experience, made the Protestant churches flourish in the country.

The Ethiopian Evangelical Church Mekane Yesus was officially founded in Addis Ababa on January 21, 1959 with 20,000 members.[3] Many mission agencies that have Lutheran and Presbyterian roots played a leading role in the process of making a national church. Since the Reformation period, there were a lot of mission works from Europe and U.S.A. to reach the people of Ethiopia with the gospel. The church is a Lutheran church: "it subscribes to Luther's small and large catechism and the Augsburg Confession."[4] The church currently has 32 synods, 8994 congregations and 4960 preaching places with a total of 10.4 million members.[5] Of these members, children and youth comprise nearly 70% of the total membership.

Prosperity Gospel in Ethiopia

The Pentecostal movement which has played a significant role in the expansion of the Protestant churches is to some extent considered as the mother of the prosperity gospel in Ethiopia. The Pentecostal movement now made substantial inroads in mainline churches like the EECMY, Kale Hiwot and even the historic Ethiopian Orthodox Tewahdo Church (EOTC). In Ethiopia, the Protestant churches are informally called *'Pente'*. This generic label to all non-EOTC and non- Catholic Christians in Ethiopia "came into usage in the late 1960s as an aftermath of an episode in Debre Zeit in August 1967… *Pente* initially referred to as the new "religious outsiders", as a shortened allusion to

---

[1] Johnny Bakke, *Christian Ministry: Patterns and Functions within the Ethiopian Evangelical Church Mekane Yesus,* Studia Missionalia Upsalinsia XLIV. Oslo: Solum Forlag A.S., 1987, p. 124.
[2] Gustav Arén, *Envoys of the Gospel in Ethiopia: In the Steps of the Evangelical Pioneers 1898-1936.* Studia Missionalia Upsaliensia LXXV. Stockholm: EFS förlaget, 1999.
[3] Fekadu Gurmesa, *Evangelical Faith Movement in Ethiopia: Origins and Establishment of the Ethiopian Evangelical Church Meakne Yesus.* Minneapolis, MN: Lutheran University Press, 2009, p. 56.
[4] Idossa Wakseyoum (ed.), *The Constitution of the Ethiopian Evangelical Church Mekane Yesus*, 2018, p. 8.
[5] 2020 Statistic of the Ethiopian Evangelical Church Mekane Yesus, Compiled by the Strategic Plan Office of the church (unpublished resource).

their Pentecostal faith experience, the most salient aspect of its expression being *speaking in tongues* as an evidence of the "baptism of the Holy Spirit."[6]

The somewhat strange nature of this experiential and expressive form of the Christian faith in Ethiopia manifested as the pejorative designation, known as *Pente,* for a movement considered not only outlandish, but also heretical. Intriguingly, the notion has remained lodged in the public imagination even to this day.

From a small and scattered beginning in the early 1960s, however, a vibrant independent Pentecostal movement eventually crystallized in the formation of the Mulu Wenegel Church, one of the most powerful agents in the diffusion of the Pentecostal experience across other non-Pentecostal denominations.[7] The name Mulu Wengel, literally, full gospel, is noteworthy because it clearly reveals the theology of Pentecostals concerning the full application of biblical accounts and promises to provide full salvation to people, physical as well as spiritual. It underscores the completeness and sufficiency of a biblically centered faith, and a church that endorses such a claim.

The prosperity gospel which has currently affected the norm and practice of the orthodox Christianity in the contemporary evangelical churches of Ethiopia, has its legacy from the Western part of the world whose theology has a blend of religion and philosophy. Writers like Bruce Barron consider Edward Erving as the first figure to propagate divine healing in the modern world.[8] However, in Ethiopia the teachings of Kenneth Hagins and Darin Prince had played a part in the formation of many independent churches like the Arinet (literally deliverance), and Rema Faith Church, to mention but two. The Rema Church of Addis Ababa had a direct link with the US office which is currently led by Kenneth W. Hagin Jr, the son of the founder. According to a research conducted by Bulutse Futuwi, "the theology of prosperity in the Rhema Faith Church in Ethiopia is the replica of the faith theology of the North American Movement."[9]

The prosperity gospel is not only non-denominational but induces a wrong method of biblical interpretation which can lead anyone that hears it to interpret the Bible in any way they like. Their churches are not filled with new converts, but with the people that come from other churches. They twist the text of the Bible in a way that call members to give money with a hope that the seed that the people sow will bring manifold heavenly blessings.

---

[6] Tibebe Eshete, *The Evangelical Movement in Ethiopia: Resistance and Resilience.* Waco, TX: Baylor University Press, 2017, p. 146.
[7] Ibid., p.147.
[8] Bruce Barron, *The Health and Wealth Gospel: What is Going on Today in a Movement that has shaped the Faith of Millions?* Downers Grove, IL: Inter Varsity Press, 1987, p. 37
[9] Bulutse Futuwi, *An Introduction to the Theology and Growth of Independent Churches in Ethiopia with Special Reference to Rema Faith Church: A critical Approach.* EGST, Unpublished M.Th. Thesis, 2002, p. 97.

The prosperity gospel considers sickness and poverty as bad and a result of lack of one's faith. If a person has faith, the blessing will not be stopped and they keep on pouring to the extent that they can flood. They teach faith as something that comes from the believer, not as something that is a gift from the Lord. However, in reality, it is the preachers that lead a well-off life which one can observe in the cars they drive, the schools that they send their children to and the houses where they live, and the expensive clothes that they wear.

Youth in Ethiopia

According to the World Health Organization (WHO), youth refers to people aged between 15 and 24 years inclusive, characterized by unique physical, psychological, social, and emotional changes that put their life at high risk. According to O"Higgins (2001), this definition may vary according to different cultural and social settings. For example, the Ethiopian Evangelical Church Mekane Yesus regards youth as persons between 18-35 years. As indicated, there is a different assumption among the developed and developing countries on the issues of youth because of the level of development and others factors. In Ethiopia the official definition of youth is those persons between the ages of 15 and 29 years.[10]

The youth have many needs that can be grouped as social,[11] emotional,[12] physical,[13] intellectual[14] and spiritual.[15] Just to unpack these needs, in an article

---

[10] The Ethiopian Federal Democratic Republic, Ministry of Youth, Sports and Culture, 2004.

[11] Social needs mean young people need healthy and stable relationships in which they can thrive. They need to feel and know that they belong. This includes functioning families, peer groups, social clubs and other relational networks. They need to belong to an interdependent community that will help them to develop socially and intellectually. In their personal development, they need to be supported by friends, mentors and role models, and at the same time be free and encouraged to make independent explorations into life.

[12] Emotional needs are the need for identity (significance, acceptance, security). Young people all over the world are desperately trying to find out who they are and what it means to be human. This search for identity includes the need to be accepted as they are, and to feel that they have a significant contribution to make. A further part of their search is the legitimate desire to have a share in real power. This includes power to shape their own personal destiny and their environment. Some also desire to have an influence and transform the realities of this world, in areas like politics, ecology and social structures.

[13] Physical needs are the basic needs (food, safety, shelter, medical care, a healthy environment) which are the same for all people. Young people are often powerless in achieving and/or securing them for themselves. Basic needs also include education and employment.

[14] Intellectual needs means young people need to be educated in order to secure better employment and other options for the future. It is frustrating for young people when parents and societal institutions do not recognize the importance of long-term

published by the academic *Journal of Agricultural Economics and Rural Development*, Dr. Abebaw Abebe lists unemployment, health and drug addiction, and migration as some of the challenges of the youth.[16] The writer of this paper also adds ethnic clashes as one of the main challenges of the youth in particular, and the nation in general.

As it is mentioned above, the EECMY's 40% of membership is youth, and these youths are not exempted from the aforementioned challenges:

- Personalizing and living out their faith
- Ethnicity
- Sexual purity in a society where pressures and temptation exists
- Personal identity and self-image issues
- Divorce and family issues
- Busyness (always involved in something)
- Absence of father figure
- Negative media influence
- Lack of discipline
- Materialism.

Effects from the Prosperity Gospel on the Youth in the EECMY

1. Leadership conflict

Youth who are very much interested in the teachings of the prosperity gospel try to propagate it to their fellow youth, and this creates problems when leaders of the congregation step in to stop it. This must be seen against the background that some elders of congregations have refused the youth to practice the unbiblical exercises, and at times close the church buildings belonging to the congregations. They youth consider the elders of the church as the Pharisees of the New Testament that were making as many attempts as possible to hamper the ministry of Jesus. Since the youth consider themselves as more spiritual that the elders, they do not consider the decisions of the elders as out of good

---

investment in education. In addition, there are regions of the world where education is not possible for all kinds of reasons.

[15] Spiritual needs means young people are searching for meaning and purpose. In many instances, this search leads them to explore alternative spiritualties and the occult, rather than the church, which often does not seem to provide viable answers, deep spiritual experience and power. In addition, there often is a disparity between the claims and message of Christians and their behaviour. Young people want to experience a transcendental reality which has the potential to infuse their lives with hope and power. They want to feel connected to something that is bigger than themselves and the realities in the world around them, which they perceive as fleeting and limiting, and sometimes outright oppressive.

[16] Abebaw Abebe, *Journal of Agricultural Economics and Rural Development*, 2020, p. 685.

motives, but as a work of the evil spirit to extinguish the fire of the Holy Spirit. This kind of act by itself at some point forces the youth to leave their congregation and migrate to the prosperity gospel churches.

2. Doctrinal clash

As the doctrinal stand of the church is against the teachings and practices of the prosperity gospel, the youth consider the church as a replica of the Western church that is close to the work of the Holy Spirit. The church is led by liturgy that has assigned particular scriptural readings. Though prosperity gospel teachers claim that they give emphasis to the word of God, their main centre of interest is experience or miracles. As a result, their teachings and preaching are far way behind the context of the Bible and the centre of the healing is against the doctrinal stand of the church. They call people to attend their programme for the 'miraculous manifestation' of the Holy Spirit, which primarily is earthly blessing or at times healing.

The church gives a high place to the Word of God and Sacraments, nothing more. In his doctoral dissertation, Rev. Tariku Tolsa, mentioned that:[17]

> This does not mean that our members that are attracted by the teachings and practices of the Charismatic Preachers have totally denied the Word of God and the Sacraments as the means that God established for us to meet him. In principle, the majority did not totally reject the importance of the Word of God and Sacraments as a means of grace. But some do not believe that Word and Sacraments are the only means by which God comes to us, for they also considered human beings with special gifts and objects like water and oil as alternative means to get access to God.

Secondly, trying to co-operate with God to receive His gifts is standing against God's independence or sovereignty. Such an attempt to co-operate with God is not a new thing for the believers of the area. Several years ago, the church's big assignment was to teach its members that salvation is possible only by grace through faith, as many did not understand that human efforts have no place in the work of salvation. There were misunderstandings and confusions among our members regarding subjects like infant baptism, until the errors were corrected through scriptural teachings that took a long time. Thus the current movement which practically undermines the importance of the divinely instituted means of grace implies that the doctrine of synergism is reviving in the area in a subtle way.

---

[17] Tariku Tolsa, *The Place and Purpose of Spiritual Gifts in the Scripture: The Understanding of the EECMY IBS Congregations in Mettu and Alge Towns.* Doctoral Dissertation, Concordia Theological Seminary, Fort Wayen, pp. 147.

3. Negative view of gospel

One of the main negative impacts that come with the prosperity gospel is to create the attitude to see the gospel as a commodity to invest upon in any way possible. This means if a person considers himself as a good preacher or as having a supernatural gift, he runs to opening a new church or ministry on which he leads and earns money from members. As a result when a new church is opened in one place, it is known as the church of the apostle or bishop or prophet someone and it is considered as a business, not for the genuine message of the gospel dissemination. As Asamoah-Gyadue puts it, this kind of Christianity has " a special attraction for Africa's upwardly mobile youth, a lay oriented leadership, ecclesiastical office based on a person's charismatic gifting, innovative use of modern media technologies, particular concern with congregational enlargements, and a relaxed and fashion-conscious dress code from members... [and] possession of material goods."[18] In short, most see the gospel as an easy ladder to wealth.

4. Improper Bible interpretation

In the modern times and especially in the context of prosperity gospel, there is misinterpretation of the Bible. In painting the Latin American picture of misinterpretation of the Bible, Salinas (2014:4) puts it this way:

> In postmodern hermeneutics, the reader has control over meaning, that is, any text can mean whatever the reader decides. Until recently, finding the author's intention has been the hermeneutical key for biblical interpretation. The idea used to be that you came to the Bible to find what God wanted to tell us, since God is the author of the Bible. However, PT has bought into today's hermeneutical tendencies. What we hear in their preaching is an imposed meaning over the text, a meaning that supports the preacher's ideas and agendas. People go to church thirsty for God's words, only to receive lies.

Sarles (1986: 339) wrote about the hermeneutics of PT teachers that leaves much to be desired. The method of interpreting the biblical text is highly subjective and arbitrary. Bible verses are quoted in abundance without attention to grammatical indicators, semantic nuances, or literary and historical context. The result is a set of ideas and principles based on a distortion of textual meaning.

The fact that the biblical author's original intent would have been plain to his original audience to whom the words were originally addressed in their context is seldom considered in PT preachers' sermons and teachings. The PT preachers read their suburbanized culture of the late 20th century setting back into the text. A survey of the volumes of literature produced by the PT teachers

---

[18] J. Kwabena Asamoah-Gyadu, *Contemporary Pentecostal Christianity: Interpretation from an African Context.* Eugene, OR: Wipf and Stock, 2013.

yields numerous examples of such misinterpretations (Jones 1998: 81). An analysis of all such examples of misinterpreted texts would fall beyond the limitations of this article.

5. Music and worship

Music facilitates the integration of daily life with the Word of God in the lives of believers within their local faith communities. As such, music serves as a life processor, a means for interacting with the biblical scriptures. It plays a central role in integrating the Christian faith within people's life context. However, this has not always been the case. The introduction of music from outside of one's culture, such as Western hymns in Africa, without understanding the new, local musical culture, led to a misunderstanding of the Christian message. The new worship style that is conducted in the churches of the prosperity gospel is affecting the choir-based worship that has been practised for many years. With a lead singer and five or six other persons, the so-called worship leaders sing at least for one and half hours. The 'worship' leaders take different famous songs that have the same musical rhythm, and usually the tempo of the music is from slow to end up with high tempo music that calls the congregants to dance, shout and jump.

Once the worship band finishes their service, many are exhausted and think the church service can be dismissed. As many programmes of the church start around 10:00 am, when the singing is done, the time reaches 12:00, and parents who came with children get many requests from children to go home for lunch.

In Ethiopian Evangelical tradition, followers of Christ are not supposed to engage in secular music. As a result, there are many youths who were expelled from the church for playing musical instruments for secular artists. Moreover, the dancing style in the worship of God and the traditional dancing are totally different. During worship, people raise their hands, bow down, kneel, but currently based on the music style of the song, we are witnessing people dancing in a traditional dance manner. Recently, a handful of prominent singers have released new music which cannot be grouped under gospel, however, this kind of music is being sung in church. Moreover, without knowing the place and the meaning of true worship, people are making the church a dance floor.

6. Wrong meaning of faith

Whereas orthodox Christianity understands faith to be trust in the person of Jesus Christ, prosperity teachers espouse something quite different: "Faith is a spiritual force, a spiritual energy, a spiritual power. It is this force of faith which makes the laws of the spirit world to function," as Copeland writes in *The Laws of Prosperity:* "There are certain laws governing prosperity revealed in God's Word. Faith causes them to function."[19] This is obviously a faulty,

---

[19] Kenneth Copeland, *The Laws of Prosperity*. Tulsa: Harrison House, 1974, p. 86.

perhaps even heretical, understanding of faith. According to prosperity theology, faith is not a God-granted, God-centred act of the will. Rather, it is a humanly wrought spiritual force, directed at God. Indeed, any theology that views faith chiefly as a means to material gain rather than justification before God must be judged inadequate at best.

Possible Guidelines to Combat the Effects of Prosperity Gospel

Embrace the Importance of Reaching and Influencing Youth with the Gospel of Jesus Christ

Reaching young people can only happen holistically. Jesus is our model and teacher. The whole gospel can bring whole healing to the millions and millions of young people within and outside of the church today. We need a new passion and urgency to understand that the time to act is now. We need to partner in prayer and concerted action, we need to train, send out and support young ambassadors for Christ to reach this generation. We need the full empowerment of the Holy Spirit.

Establish Relationships as the Core of all Ministry and Outreach to Youth

The great needs of young people span the entire spectrum of human needs. The need for relationship is central for all and needs to be understood as such. Relevant relationships, lived out in authentic and tangible community, are the foundation stones for all true and effective ministry. Building relationships with young people demands time and real interest, steadfastness and a servant attitude. At the same time, there is the need for boldness and spiritual authority which stem from a reliance on the Lord Jesus Christ, a renewed trust in God's Word and the power of the Holy Spirit in the fellowship of the church

Engage with the Real Needs of Young People in Culturally Relevant Ways

To reach the young generation with the liberating news of Jesus Christ, we need to go beyond our comfort zones to meet them where they are, and accept them as they are. We need to understand deeply all issues related to the real needs of young people, and to seek to develop answers that are relevant both culturally and spiritually. Mission to young people is in many cases a cross-cultural venture, and must be undertaken in the spirit of humility, teach ability and sensibility which characterize every true service in the name of Jesus, who took on a servant's form for our sake. At the same time we must be bold to engage the powers of darkness that try to destroy God's purposes for the young generation. Mission to young people remains under the promise which Jesus made to his followers: "I am with you always until the ends of the earth."

Equip the Children and Youth Ministers

The statistic of the church shows that the numbers of pastors and evangelists of the church are 14059 (4410 pastors and 9649).[20] The numbers of pastors are nearly 5000 which is half of the numbers of the congregation and the preaching places (8994 congregations and 4960 preaching places) together. Most of the activities of the church are executed by 763,156 laities or volunteers. This is mainly due to the huge membership growth that happens as a result of summer evangelism works of the congregations. Big congregations that are situated in the big cities have started hiring full-time children and youth ministers, but most of these full-time ministers are either graduates of theology or social studies. Moreover, most of the time, the elders council which administers the works of the congregational works gives more attention to constructing buildings other than ways to equip the ministers or the youth. If the issues of the youth are not dealt with, it can open doors for them to go out from one church, and this leads to migration of youth from one place to another, or dissatisfaction with their minister and elders. Recently the Mekane Yesus Seminary together with the children and youth ministry of the church have prepared a curriculum for children and youth ministry study at undergraduate level. This is a good start, but all the nine regional seminaries and the 51 Bible Schools of the church must start courses that can well equip their students toward the ministry of the youth.

Boost Media Use in the Church

The prosperity theology propagating churches are effective in media and publications. They inject a lot of money on this part of their ministry. Their YouTube channels are the one that have so many viewers that they generate 4-5000 dollars per week. The media that the church is using which can be expressed in the tv and radio programmes need to shape the structure in a way that can produce teachings that can grab the attention of the youth and address their challenges.

Readjusting Administrative Works

Mainstream faith churches should improve their rigid administrative factors that seem not to conform to the expectations of the youth, put in place mentorship programmes, give youth opportunities, and incorporate some of the attractive features in other churches instead of leaders fearing being overtaken by the youth who desire to have opportunities to explore their talents and potential.

---

[20] 2019 Statistic of the Ethiopian Evangelical Church Mekane Yesus.

Government Involvement in Bringing Responsible Youth

There is further need for the government to take responsibility of the common needs of the youth in the market places, cost effective education, and constructive social hall meetings for inspirational and motivational speakers to nurture the all-round optimistic citizens in this 21st century. And the youth's plans and policies should be implemented into actions.

Encourage to Work

From the point of view of sociology, it is known that wealth and success in general contribute towards a high social status. An analysis of group dynamics also shows that people in general tend to listen more to, and tend to congregate more around, the affluent than ordinary lowly members of society. In any case, both the Old Testament and the New Testament give testimony to this fact that it is difficult to control and to lead while in dire poverty. The first direct command to the human being in Genesis 1:26ff to "have dominion over creation" is based on the wisdom appended onto it, and that is to "be fruitful and multiply". In the New Testament, we see the Church spreading with the aid of affluent members of society, the likes of Gaius who owned a plaza and in whose house the church congregated. There is no question about it that the church, like any social institution, requires financial resources. The church can encourage members to work very hard and support its mission.

Conclusion

In conclusion, the EECMY must take a leading role in putting strategies to equip the youth members, so that they can be light and salt to the nation in particular and the world in general. Otherwise, the theology of the prosperity gospel, which is sneaking into the heart of the youth, will take them away from the church and Christ.

PART TWO

Biblical and Theological Reflection on Wealth and Prosperity in Africa

Divine Blessing in Deuteronomy 28:15
Nicodeme Alagbada

The careful reader of the book of Deuteronomy cannot fail to realise that this book is composed of the summary of Israel's experiences in the desert, followed by the development of some fundamental laws mentioned in the previous books, and a series of prophecies following the unfolding history of this people freed from slavery in Egypt until the time of their settlement in Palestine. This is why one can easily see that the book of Deuteronomy looks to the past, and opens onto the future at the same time.[1] This fifth book of the scroll called the Torah is entitled in Hebrew *"Debarim"* (Words), and Deuteronomy (Second Law), according to the Septuagint (LXX) and the Vulgate. Covering the large section composed of Joshua, Judges, Samuel, Kings, the book of Deuteronomy is mainly devoted to the speeches of Moses, delivered a little before his death in the plains of Moab facing Palestine, addressed to an audience a little different from the community of the first 40 years of liberation of the Israelite people.

Starting with a series of exhortations and memories of the conquests, wars and sufferings endured, this book emphasises the love of God and his multidimensional protection on the one hand, and the obedience of man and the exhortation to keep the clauses of the covenant made at Sinai in order to avoid the wrath of a jealous God, on the other hand. On these two concepts, the love of God and obedience (listening and putting into practice the voice of God), depend divine blessing and the possession of wealth which are discussed in our essay of theological reflection on Deuteronomy 28: 1-5. Is the possession of physical and material wealth synonymous with divine blessing? Is it activated by faith and obedience to the Word of God, or by the gifts and offerings that the believer brings to God or invests in the church?

The Bible repeatedly affirms that God is rich in goodness while also showing that believers face various trials, privations, and temptations through which they are called to grow in faith. Unfortunately, this point of view is not shared by some theologians of prosperity. Evangelists and pastors of this theological current, messengers of happiness, base their views on some biblical texts and ideologies, to capture uninformed or misguided people by preaching to them the God of prosperity, which is not a deviance in itself. But through well-directed messages such as, *"Give... God will repay you a hundred times over, Put your faith in action... and you will be healed! Whoever sows*

---

[1] Deuteronomy 8.2; 6.10; 8.7; 30.1-5.

sparingly will also reap sparingly, Each one will reap what he will have sown or even, *The gold and silver are mine, says the Lord"*, these messengers maintain an unbiblical amalgam by putting material, physical and spiritual prosperity at the same label. Yet, is it not obvious that the possession of physical and material wealth is not synonymous with divine blessing? Therefore, our contribution to the theological reflection on Deuteronomy 28.1-5 consists in proposing a warning on the excesses of the prosperity theology, by establishing the relationship between divine blessing and the possession of wealth. In an approach that is at the same time historical, analytical, explanatory and suggestive, this contribution focuses on two points. The first point is "Analysis, explanation and significance of Deuteronomy 28.1-5 in the perspective of the prosperity theology", and the second is "From divine blessing to the possession of wealth: a warning on the drifts of the prosperity theology".

Analysis, explanation and significance of Deuteronomy 28.1-5 from the perspective of Prosperity Theology

From all the research on the book of Deuteronomy, it should be remembered that this book is not a simple repetition or recapitulation of the covenant laws or clauses mentioned in the books of Exodus, Leviticus, and Numbers. Its contents obviously show that it is *a second presentation of the law aimed at members of the new generation*[2] ready to settle in the Promised Land. Taken as a whole, the book is attributed to Moses as author, according to tradition. However, liberal criticism or historical-critical study, noting that the death of Moses is mentioned in the last chapter, speculates that the book might have been written by Moses around 1407-1406 BCE, except the last part which might have probably written by Joshua after the death of Moses.[3] History also reveals that this *Book of the Law* was discovered during the time of King Josiah, the reformer, in 620 BCE.

In its structure, the book of Deuteronomy is composed of four speeches[4] of Moses (1-4; 5-26; 27-28; 29-30) and a conclusion grouping together the last words of Moses and the account of his death (31-34). Chapters 27 and 28 raise questions related to blessings or curses resulting from obedience or disobedience. These two chapters (27-28) are placed between the reminder of the laws of Sinai, warnings, exhortations (5-26) and the alliance with Israel for

---

[2] William MacDonald, Arthur Farstad, *Le commentaire biblique Ancien Testament du disciple*, Romanel-sur-Lausanne: Société Biblique de Genève, 2010, p. 194.
[3] *La Bible avec notes d'étude, Vie nouvelle, Segond 21*, Romanel-sur-Lausanne: Société Biblique de Genève, 2009, p. 260.
[4] The first discourse: Deuteronomy 1:4.43; the second discourse: Deuteronomy 4:44-28.68; the third discourse: Deuteronomy 28.69-30.20; the fourth discourse: Deuteronomy 30-32.

the Promised Land, warnings and blessings (29-30). This visible ranking is not insignificant. It allows the reader to have a logical continuation of the conditions and moral values of living differently that must be the impact of the covenant of God on Israel, a people freed from the Pharaonic yoke of Egypt for a new life. When they arrive in the land that God had promised them, the people of Israel will have to engrave the law received at Sinai on stones at Mount Ebal and build an entirely stone-made altar on which they will be offering thanksgiving sacrifices (27.1-8). This periscope indicates the blessings and curses to be pronounced on Mounts Garizim and Ebal (27.9-26), the conditions of blessing (28.1-14) and the consequences of curse (28.15-68). Thus, the book of Deuteronomy in this part recalls reminds people that the happiness to which every person aspires is found essentially in constant or permanent obedience to the liberating God.

Also, the peculiarity of Deuteronomy 28 is that with chapter 29, this chapter relates to the divine covenant made with Israel for the Promised Land and formulated in chapter 30:1-9. This covenant concerning the Promised Land provides for seven steps:

 a. Dispersal due to disobedience (Deuteronomy 28.63-68; 30.1);
 b. Israel's future repentance during the dispersal (Deuteronomy 30.2);
 c. Return of the Lord (Deuteronomy 30:3; Amos 9:9-15);
 d. Return to the country (Deuteronomy 30:5; Isaiah 11:11-13; Ezekiel 37:21-25);
 e. National conversion (Deuteronomy 30: 6; Hosea 2; 16-18);
 f. Judgment of the oppressors of Israel (Deuteronomy 30:7; Joel 3:1-8);
 g. National prosperity (Deuteronomy 30:9; Amos 9.11-15).

Explanation and Significance of Deuteronomy 28.1-5

Do you understand what you are reading? ... How can I understand unless someone explains it to me?[5] These two questions asked respectively by Philippe and the Ethiopian are an illustration of the need to understand, and above all, to better understand what we read. This is what we will try to explain in this sub-section. In reconsidering our periscope in its context, we give ourselves as an exercise the clarification of these first five verses of Deuteronomy 28, in order to make them understandable both in the overall context of the book of Deuteronomy, and that of the possession of wealth which is our challenge.

Indeed, before settling in the Promised Land, the new generation of the people of Israel inevitably needed a renewal of the covenant. This renewal of the covenant requires recalling the story of the departure from Egypt operated by Moses under the direction and control of the God of Israel. The history of

---

[5] Acts of the Apostles 8:30-31.

this liberation is marked by the powerful interventions of God and the disobedience of the people. Thus, there is the need for the repetition of the law of God's love and faithfulness manifested to his people. In so doing, the people are faced with a critical choice between the path of obedience for the covenant to be ratified and for receiving the blessing, and the path of rebellion against the law of God leading to disaster. The people of Israel have an obligation to love the Lord their God, not to forget him and to remain faithful to him, hence the phrase *remember and do not forget.* This obligation is due to the fact that it is out of sheer grace that this people is chosen from among other nations. This faith of Israel in one God, the liberating God, calls for strict observance of the Lord's commandments. It is in this context of covenant[6] for the Promised Land, revealing the conditions of entry into Canaan, that it is necessary, on the one hand, to situate the six blessings of Deuteronomy 28[7] and understand, on the other hand, the periscope we chose (Deuteronomy 28.1-5).

Verses 1-14 speak of blessings resulting from obedience, while the rest of the chapter (verses 15-68), describes curses as consequences of disobedience and forsaking of the Lord by His people. Among the blessings cited in the chosen periscope we note: the pre-eminence or superiority of Israel among the nations which will result in material prosperity, fruitfulness, soil fertility, an abundance of crops, victory in battle, and success in international trade. In modern terms, all these formulated blessings have as a target, from the first verse, Israel's national dignity and its glory based on strict obedience to divine commandments.

a. Listening (Shema שָׁמַע)

We consider the edited Hebrew text (Masoretic Text) as such to translate our pericope. So the first verse could be translated as:

> And it will happen that (וְהָיָה), if you diligently listen (אִם־שָׁמוֹעַ תִּשְׁמַע) to the voice (בְּקוֹל) of the LORD your God, seeing to practice (לִשְׁמֹר לַעֲשׂוֹת) all his commandments (אֶת־כָּל־מִצְוֺתָיו) that I give today, then the LORD your God will make you superior (עֶלְיוֹן) to all the nations of the earth (הָאָרֶץ)

Listening is a theme that often comes up in the book of Deuteronomy with repeated formulae. So, in this book, the imperative, *"Listen"*, addressed to Israel, is found six times.[8] In this verse, which can be considered as an

---

[6] The main covenants made in the Old Testament are: Covenant in Eden (Genesis 2:16); Covenant with fallen Adam (Genesis 3:15); Covenant with Noah (Genesis 9:16); Covenant with Abram (Genesis 12:2); Covenant of Sinai (Exodus 19:5); Covenant with David (2 Samuel 7:16).
[7] This chapter 28 of the book of Deuteronomy matches Leviticus 26. Together they constitute a double and solemn testimony warning the people of Israel about the outcomes of their obedience or disobedience.
[8] See Deuteronomy 4: 1; 5.1; 6: 4; 9: 1; 20: 3; 27: 9.

introduction to the whole chapter 28 of Deuteronomy, we can remember that the attention of the new generation of Israel is focused on the fact that the rise to social and national dignity is a divine blessing linked to listening to («שָׁמַע »Shāmaʻ) the voice (the Word) of the God of Israel, and ensuring that his commandments are put into practice. Hearing is the most important sense for the Israelite in the Bible, unlike the Greek of the Middle East for whom the most important sense is sight.[9]

The verbs, to observe, or, to make sure to put into practice, express here the meaning of the verb " שָׁמַע " (Shāmaʻ), generally translated into English as "to listen". According to the context, biblical equivalents of this verb שָׁמַע can mean to hear, to obey, to answer, to perceive, to learn, to understand, to discern. In the book of Deuteronomy, listening is one of the characteristics of a living being who is able to enter into a personal relationship. It is a manifestation of the ability to enter into dialogue with others and with God. In the Bible, especially in the Old Testament, God reveals himself as God who speaks and invites people to listen. But, He is also the one who is challenged, consulted, and, therefore, required to listen. As a matter of fact, those who listen to the voice of God can bring about obedience to God by ensuring that they carry out His ordinances or commandments. Therefore, the verb, 'to listen', can sometimes be translated as 'to obey' (See Deuteronomy 5:27). The priest, the king, the prophet as well as the people of Israel as a whole, are invited to listen attentively in their relationship with God. This attentive and diligent listening is just the obedience which is the way for the people to welcome the covenant that God makes with them. It is like a condition for the validity and durability of this covenant.[10] Through listening-obedience to the voice of God, the people open themselves to the happiness with which God wants to bless them. This happiness is available, but the people still have to seize it and appropriate it by means of listening and obedience. It is at this level that we point out the relevance of the place of שָׁמַע in the practice of divine commandments aimed at making Israel elevated or superior to all the nations in the world. If the people of Israel listen to their God, they will appear wise and discerning. They will be admired by other nations. When they call on their God, he will listen to, and deliver them. In this context, listening means answering and fulfilling (See Deuteronomy 26: 7-8). The answer is a proof of this listening. In this regard, one can, depending on the context, translate "to listen" as "to answer". Listening, therefore, becomes a reciprocal attitude or an inclusive dialogue. Listening is also an attitude of adherence to God. This explains the imperative *"Listen Israel",* with the goal of the happiness of Israel and its elevation above other nations. Following all the senses of listening, we can come back to our periscope to stress that the key to the

---

[9] https://fr.m.wikipedia.org/wiki/%C3%89coute_(th%C3%A8me-biblique, consulted on 1st November, 2020.
[10] See Deuteronomy 7: 12; 8: 20.

uplifting of Israel, its prosperity or its riches, is without any doubt its listening-obedience.

b. Elyôn (עֶלְיוֹן God Most High)

One of the effects of listening-obedience to the voice of God is *Elyôn*, an attribute of God frequently used in Judaism and the Bible.[11] God's purpose was for Israel to be above all the nations, that is to make Israel superior to all the nations of the earth, to raise it to the glory of God, or to the rank of God on the sole condition that it listens to the voice (בְּקוֹל) of God by keeping the commandments prescribed to this nation by Moses. This verse 1 of Deuteronomy 28 allows us to note here that it is not the possession of physical or material wealth that elevates a nation. Elevation is rather brought about by the obedience to God reflected in the practice of His will, or of His plan for humanity. Therefore, the teaching of prosperity theology should be focused on listening to the voice of God, and practising His commandments, and not on the quest for the acquisition of money and the possession of material goods. In this regard, Jesus' warning deserves to be emphasized here: *Beware of all greed, for the life of a man does not depend on his goods, even though he is in abundance (Luke 12:15)*. Greed is the pursuit of possessions, and the anxious maintaining of what one has. This warning here is not to regard the acquisition of goods as a bad thing in itself because the essential thing is the positive use of them.

Divine Blessings and Possession of Wealth:
Warning on the Drift of Prosperity Theology

Blessings (הַבְּרָכוֹתhaberâkôt)

And all these blessings (kal-haberakotכָּל־הַבְּרָכוֹת) will be yours, if you listen to the voice of the Lord your God. You will be blessed in the city, and you will be blessed in the fields. The Lord will bless you with many children, with abundant crops, and with many cattle and sheep. The Lord will bless your corn crops, and the food you prepare from them. (Deuteronomy 28.2-5)

Verses 2-5 of our periscope show the blessings that reflect the superiority or elevation of Israel as its people listen to the voice of the Lord their God. Being attentive is the key to any success, because it consists of being present and available to feel and act accordingly, quietly and effectively. Receiving God's

---

[11] André-Marie Gerard *Elyôn*, in: *Dictionnaire de la Bible*. Paris: Robert Laffont, 1989, p. 321. R.-Ferdinand Poswick (dir.), Guy Rainotte (dir.), *Élyôn*, in: Dictionnaire de la Bible et des 3 religions du Livre. Paris: Lidis, 1985, p. 170.

voice requires sustained attention that results in consistent action, providing access to divine blessing as the source of true prosperity that is not reduced to the possession of material goods.

In the Bible, the Hebrew term most often translated by the verb to bless is *barak,* whose derivative is *b^erakah,* blessing (בְּרָכָה). The verb *barak* (to bless) can also mean praise, congratulate or greet or even curse.[12] The subject of this verb is either God or man. For example, in Genesis 1:22, God blesses birds and sea animals by calling them to be fertile and to multiply on the face of the earth. The same blessing is given to Adam and Eve. God also gives them dominion over all creation.

In the case of Abram called by God to go to the Promised Land (Genesis 12: 1-3), God promised to bless him, to make his name great, and to bless all the families of the earth through him. Obviously, these blessings are clearly linked to happiness and prosperity for Abram, who became Abraham, and for others. According to Genesis 22:16-18, Abraham was blessed again by God. This time, God specifies that this blessing is due to Abraham's obedience to His voice. The divine blessings pronounced on Abraham are clearly linked to happiness and prosperity, for himself and for others. In fact, at the beginning of creation, God's purpose or will for creation was that His creatures, including the humanity, have prosperity, peace and fullness.

From all the above, it should be remembered that *b^erakah* (בְּרָכָה) is a divine act, a wish of kindness and happiness for someone else, possibly with a condition for its fulfilment. The will of God is the good of the human being created in His image and likeness. In the Bible, *b^erakah* (בְּרָכָ = blessing) is used 53 times in the Old Testament, and 14 times in the New Testament. Depending on the contexts in which it is used, it can have three meanings: a grace bestowed by God, a human wish that God will act favourably towards someone else and the joy of one who sees the success or happiness of others. It is through the last two meanings that we find that *b^erakah* (בְּרָכָה = blessing) can also be given or pronounced by human beings. Among many examples, we can mention the cases of the patriarchs Abraham, Isaac and Jacob, who blessed their sons in order to transmit to them the blessing which they themselves received from God. We can also mention the nuptial blessing that Rebecca received from her family before leaving to join her husband Isaac.[13]

In the framework of good manners or improved condition, blessing is not just courtesy, but a wish that God restore his favour for somebody, or an affirmation of his inherent kindness. But, in their walk with God, humans, through the Israelite people, fail to stay with diligence in listening to the voice of God by making sure to practice his commandments.

---

[12] https://www.gotquestions.org/Français/benediction-Bible.html, consulted on 30th October, 2020

[13] Genesis 24.60: Become the ancestor of millions of people and may your descendants own the cities of their enemies!

Possession of Wealth

I have riches and glory, durable goods and justice (Proverbs 8:18).

God's blessing makes you wealthy. Hard work can make you no richer (Proverbs 10:22).

The Bible attests that wealth or earthly material goods are given by God and they are signs of God's favour granted to those who fear Him and walk in His way. It also states that they are proofs of divine protection. Thriving flocks and fertile lands are blessings from God. Indeed, *Abram was a very rich man, with sheep, goats, and cattle, as well as silver and gold,* according to Genesis 13: 2. Also in the Bible, several Hebrew words are rendered by the term wealth. These are *nekâsim* (possessions), *hôn* (goods, acquired fortune), *khaïl* (opulence) and *tôb* (well-being, prosperity). In addition, in Deuteronomy 28: 2-5, God proposes to open his good treasure to the people of Israel when they settle in the Promised Land.

These divine blessings include pre-eminence among the nations, material prosperity, fruitfulness, soil fertility, abundance of crops, victory in battle, and success in international trade.[14] *At the time of patriarchs and long after, wealth was constituted by the size of herds, the number of head of cattle, and servants owned by the clan or the head of the family.*[15] It, therefore, seems obvious that God is not against wealth or the possession of wealth which is the result of the people's listening and obedience to His voice. Moreover, if God grants temporal blessings to His people, he undoubtedly pursues a spiritual goal which consists in making His people understand that He is the God of prosperity, who elevates and lowers, who enriches and impoverishes, who grants blessings and who removes them. Therefore, Israel must understand that its true wealth is God himself.

However, according to Psalms 73: 4, 12,[16] material riches are not just the divine reward given to those who do good. Here, Asaph testifies to the perplexity he feels at seeing the prosperity of the wicked who do not listen to the voice of God, and do not make sure to carry out His commandments. This

---

[14] From the time of kings, commerce became a source of wealth, in addition to breeding and agriculture. At that time, the country of Israel was located at the crossroads of the great trade routes between Egypt and Asia. This privileged location promoted its socio-economic development. A new conception of wealth also became commonplace, supporting the notion of wealth not based on production, but on exchange.

[15] https://topbible.topchretien.com/dictionnaire/richesse,consulted on 11th February, 2020

[16] Ps. 73.4, 12 (TOB): *They do not deny themselves anything up to their death, they are strong and healthy. That is what the wicked are like. They have plenty and are always getting more.*

Psalm 73, like this excerpt from Jeremiah 12: 1-2,[17] emphasises that possession of wealth or prosperity is not always a sign of divine blessing, much less of his approval. *Therefore, those who teach that a Christian must always live in prosperity distort the meaning of Scriptures.*[18] *For reputation is better than great wealth, and grace is better than silver and gold* (Proverbs 22.1). Here, prosperity theologians must realize that material prosperity or the possession of wealth is not obligatory when one is a believer, and that it is a deviance to lead or invite those who go through poverty to think that they are excluded from the love of God. In the same way, they should avoid arousing in the hearts of believers either revolt against God, or the illusion of the commercialization of divine blessings. Should not the greatest wealth as well as the greatest good of believers consist in approaching God on whom depends all reality, the Sovereign, Lord of Israel, who promised to be Providence and Protector of His people if they listen to His voice, making sure they put His commandments into practice?

What to remember?

This essay about theological reflection on Deuteronomy 28:1-5 has enabled us to answer this question of faith in the face of prosperity theology: if God blesses those who obey Him, why do we see those whose hearts are far from Him prosper, while righteous and honest people suffer poverty and oppression? In most Bible texts, as confirmed by verses 1-5 of Deuteronomy 28, it is said that those who find pleasure in the law of God prosper, but those who deviate from it indulge in the curse. The contrast is striking when one sees the happiness of those who disobey the voice of God. The possession of wealth in this perspective cannot be a sign of divine blessing. The believer's happiness and prosperity are not in material possessions, but in the presence and closeness of God.

Divine blessings are aimed at the spiritual prosperity of the believers who draw near to God by listening to His voice and by their obedience to His commandments. They do not aim at the possession of riches that do not last and would prevent believers from leading a productive life characterized by the fruit of the Spirit: love, joy, peace, patience, kindness, goodness, faithfulness, humility, and self-control. So, whoever listens to the voice of God while ensuring to practise His commandments, accepts to be a witness of divine blessings among those around Him.

---

[17] Jer. 12: 1-2 (TOB) *Lord, if I argued my case with you, you would prove to be right. Yes, I must question you about matters of justice. Why are the wicked so prosperous? Why do dishonest people succeed? You plant them and they take root; they grow and bear fruit. They always speak well of you, yet they do not really care about you.*
[18] https://topmessage.topchrétien.com/serie-texte/lueurs-du-matin/la-prosperite-des-mechants-1/, consulted on 04 November 2020

The divine blessings promised to the people of Israel if they obey the voice of God, namely pre-eminence among the nations, material prosperity, fruitfulness, soil fertility, abundance of crops, victory in battle and success in international trade, consist in strengthening the covenant that God made with these people. Departing from this understanding of the purposes of divine blessings, prosperity theology, presented as a teaching based on the possession of wealth such as the acquisition of money and material goods, cannot fail to have a negative influence on genuine Christian faith.

Positive Relationship between Economics and Theology
Abednego Nkamuhabwa Keshomshahara

African Churches are ministering in the context of many theological challenges, among which are complexities of theologies of poverty, wealth and prosperity. Some people glorify poverty as a precondition to inherit the Kingdom of God, while others glorify wealth as a product of faith or a sign of being elected by God for everlasting life. The spiritualization of material poverty has a negative attitude towards wealth and rich people, hence, a hindrance to poverty reduction or creation of wealth. On the other hand, glorification of wealth as a proof of having faith or sign of being saved by God leads to a judgmental attitude towards the poor, as people who are predestined to failures, miseries and hell.

Biblical social ethics does not hate wealth; rather it is against wealth that is obtained through exploitation, oppression and greed.[1] The negative attitude towards wealth and poverty demands for a positive relationship between theology and economics so that Christians may relate well to issues of production, distribution and consumption of goods so as to create wealth in a way that neither exploit others, nor abuse religion for personal interests.

At the same time, wealth ought to be seen as a means towards an end rather than an end in itself. This can help churches in Africa to view wealth and prosperity as means for realizing God's Kingdom or honouring God, rather than being a proof of having faith in God or a sign of being predestined to everlasting life. The perception of wealth as means towards an end leads to co-operation between the rich and poor in the whole process of poverty reduction. This paper, therefore, discusses the complexities of theologies of poverty, wealth and prosperity in Africa by addressing the theological challenges of spiritualizing material poverty and wealth, while proposing a positive relationship between theology and economics as one of the solutions.

---

[1] Von Traugott Roser und Renate Zitt, "Vom Monolog zum Dialog, von soziale Tat zu Ordnung: zur Beziehung zwischen Theologie und Oekonomie." In Daniel Dietzfelbinger and Jochen Teuffel (eds). *Heils-Okonomie:Zum zusammenwirken von Kirche und Wirtschaft.* Guetersloh: Chr. Kaiser Guetehrsloher Verlagshaus, 2002, pp. 15-45.

Spiritualization of Material Poverty as a Hindrance to Poverty Reduction

There has been a problem of wrongly interpreting Luke 6:20 where the poor people are viewed as the blessed ones who will inherit the Kingdom of God. This understanding misleads people to the spiritualization of material poverty as a way of salvation. It can also make the poor be inactive in the struggle of eradicating poverty and miserable conditions they face in their lives. Moreover, this perception can lead to a negative attitude towards wealth and rich people. The same applies to a negative attitude towards economics as worldly or ungodly, hence making some Christians and churches fail to benefit from the principles of economics that would help churches and Christians to pursue their goals by means of management of financial, human and material resources plus the advantages of planning, implementation and evaluation of church activities for development of church institutions, Christians and communities at large.[2]

The text of Luke 6:20 is not clear on the type of poverty which is referred to. At least Mathew 5:3 is clear on the type of poverty which is meant in the beatitudes, that is being poor in spirit. Hence, the beatitudes categorically refer to spiritual poverty of depending on God.[3] This indicates that both the poor and the rich people are challenged to depend on God entirely. As such, material poverty is not a precondition to inherit God's Kingdom. Material poverty ought to be combated for the well-being of humans without being praised as a way of salvation.

The Challenge of Glorifying Wealth as a Sign of Inheriting the Kingdom of God and having Faith in God

While prosperity is good, it should not be seen as a necessary product of faith. Also it should not be regarded as an end in itself, but rather as a means towards the end. It should not be glorified; rather it should be for the glory of God. A Good Samaritan gives us a good example when he uses his wealth like oil and wine to heal the wounds of the injured person, takes him to hospital and pays his money to take care of him (Luke 10:25-37). In this way, wealth becomes a means towards realization of the Kingdom of God, His love and diaconal spirit for the needy. Thus, wealth can be used by Christians and the church to pursue church goals, as long as wealth is obtained fairly.

We experience churches which teach and preach that being prosperous and successful is a sign of having faith in God, being saved or being predestined to eternal life. As Bradley Koch observes, such views have been somehow shaped by Lutheranism and Calvinism based on Max Weber's analysis of the

---

[2] Abednego Keshomshahara, *A Theology of Poverty Reduction in Tanzania: A Quest for Socio- Economic and Political Vision.* Dodoma: CTP, 2008, pp. 244-248.
[3] Faustine Mahali, *The Concept of Poverty in Luke from the Perspective of the Wanji of Tanzania.* Arusha: Makumira, 2006, p. 12.

Protestant ethic that led to Western capitalism.[4] Luther perceived work as a spiritual calling, hence leading to hard working and a positive attitude to wealth that partly contributed to Western capitalism as Max Weber observes.[5]

Again, Calvinism stressed the doctrine of predestination, whereby Calvin's followers taught that the sign of being predestined to inheritance of God's Kingdom is being prosperous. Such teachings made Calvin's followers economize their living expenditure by abstaining from luxurious life so as to maintain their sign of being elected by God to inherit eternal life. In this way, they accumulated wealth. As a result, as Max Weber observed, Protestantism partly contributed to the rise of capitalism in Western Europe.[6] Thus, Lutheranism and Calvinism benefited the followers unlike the prosperity gospel that benefits the church leaders in most cases.

Lutheranism and Calvinism were not concerned with giving in order to prosper when they dealt with working hard and predestination theology; rather they were concerned with serving God and His people (Luther), and trying to know who are predestined to inherit the Kingdom of God (followers of Calvin). Their teachings led to prosperity, while their aim was not prosperity. Propagators of the prosperity gospel connect faith to prosperity and select biblical texts and interpret them in a way that persuades Christians to give more for their personal economic gains, not for the glory of God, but mainly for church leaders who prosper at the expense of their followers.

Relating faith to prosperity becomes a problem, especially when some people who have no Christian faith prosper even more than those who have Christian faith. It is sad to note that countries where the gravity of Christianity is found nowadays are at the same time poor countries.[7] This poses a precaution on thinking that having faith automatically leads to prosperity. The words of Jesus should be taken seriously when he said that God mercifully takes care of good and bad people, righteous and unrighteous ones (Mathew.5:44-45). While religion or faith can be one of the factors that can lead to prosperity, we ought to know that there are other factors, non-religious ones, that lead to the creation of wealth or prosperity.

The human desire to prosper has been used to mislead people, when Christians are told to pray only and wait for miracles without working hard.[8] As a result, some Christians have had illusory hopes instead of having what Ernest

---

[4] Bradley A. Koch, "The Prosperity Gospel and Economic Prosperity: Race, Class, Giving, and Voting." Ph.D. Thesis, Indiana University, 2009, pp. 11-13.
[5] Keshomshahara, *A Theology of Poverty Reduction,* pp. 214-215.
[6] Ibid., pp. 11-13.
[7] Ibid., pp. 1-2.
[8] Keshomshahara, 'Kazi za Roho Mtakatifu na Changamoto za Siku hizi' in *Semina ya Kiroho: Maombi, Miujiza na Kazi za Roho Mtakatifu dhidi ya Changamoto za Siku hizi* ("Works of the Holy Spirit and current Challenges" in Spiritual Seminar on Prayers, Miracles and Works of the Holy Spirit against the current Challenges**).** Mwanza: Godwin Gunewe, 2017, p. 43.

Bloch calls a 'militant hope' that struggles to realize the hopes in the present life realities.⁹ Such people who pray only and fail to struggle and realize their dreams, fail to know that the one who told Christians to pray, is the one who told them to seek, knock and struggle for success in their lives (Mathew 7:7). Others are told to pray only without going to hospital, in other cases students are told to pray without studying hard, hoping to experience miracles.

Illusory hopes in religion made some critics of religion to view religion as a man-made institution for the projection of human wishes, in the sense that man creates God in his mind to comfort him/herself (Ludwig Feuerbach). Sigmund Freud, like Feuerbach, regarded religion as childish wishes and illusions that must be cured psychologically. Other critics of religion said that religion is the opium of the people that gives them temporary good feelings while in reality the problems remain unsolved.

In the same line of argument, Ernest Bloch, a philosopher who studied Marxism and Christianity at the same time, was not happy with irresponsible Christians who do not play their part in their struggle, hoping that God would do everything for them. He reached the extent of radically urging the Christians to build the Kingdom of God without God. He viewed Jesus as a human being who called himself God so that his followers should not look at God in heaven for everything, but look at themselves as God on earth, as actors in solving their problems. Hence, for him, the Kingdom of God should be the kingdom of man on earth not in heaven.¹⁰

However, while Juergen Moltmann accepts the argument that religion should deal with socio-economic and political aspects of life, he challenges Ernest Bloch and other critics of religion to think beyond this world. He says that they should also consider human spiritual needs and God's intervention in human history for the total salvation of humans. He challenges Feuerbach and Karl Marx for their positive attitude towards humans as capable of building a good society and humanity. Moltmann reveals another reality about humans, whereby history has shown that human beings are oppressors, exploiters, brutal, cruel and destructors of nature. Hence, there is a need for religion, in our case Christianity, which gives hope for the present life conditions, and hope beyond this world. Thus, religion should address human needs for better life, forgiveness, and overcoming meaninglessness, pain, limitations and death through the resurrection of Jesus.¹¹

In a similar way, Christopher Dawson in his book which is about progress and religion, shows how religion and spirituality are part and parcel of the development and civilization of society. He argues that we cannot avoid religion in matters pertaining to development. He contends that:

---

⁹ Keshomshahara, *A Theology of Poverty Reduction*, p. 174ff.
¹⁰ Ibid., pp. 170 -176.
¹¹ Ibid., pp. 170 -178.

> Every living culture must possess some spiritual dynamic, which provides the energy necessary for that sustained social effort which is civilization. Normally, this dynamic is supplied by a religion, but in exceptional circumstances, the religious impulse may disguise under philosophical or political forms... Sociologists in the past have tended to disregard or minimize the social functions of religion... it is true, as I believe, that every culturally vital society must possess a religion, whether explicit or disguised, and that the religion of the society determines to a great extent its cultural form, it is obvious that the whole problem of social development and change must be studied anew in relation to the religious factor.[12]

In view of the above insight, in the context where the society has many religions and denominations, there is a need of scrutinizing the religious views to see if those views are leading people towards development or misleading people towards failure and destruction. We witness Christians in Africa who are cheated when they are told to receive cars while praying, and act as if they are driving those cars inside the church building. In other cases, such poor people are told to offer money before prayers are made for immediate wealth. The teachings of Jesus that, "you have received freely, freely give (Mathew 10:8), are no longer adhered to in the prosperity gospel. Unfortunately, when prayers are not answered positively, they are normally told that they have no faith in God, which is why they do not succeed in prayers. The same applies to those who suffer from diseases or fail to achieve their goals. This is because the prosperity gospel does not accept the other realities of suffering, dying, and failures in human lives.

Others are told that their failures are caused by curses from their relatives. Such teachings add more problems to the poor since they will waste much of their time and money in consulting either traditional doctors or church leaders on how to ward off curses. In most cases, the poor's money is further taken before consultation or prayers are made. This adds more poverty to the poor people. Such teachings should take seriously Galatians 3:13, where Paul says that the death of Jesus on the cross took away all the curses, hence we have to believe in Jesus Christ who defeated the powers of curses and sins through his sacrifice on the cross.

The prosperity gospel is challenged not to associate every failure with lack of faith in God, or wickedness. A good example is Jesus Christ, who prayed in Gethsemane to be saved from torture and death, but he respected the will of God to be done (Mark 14: 32-56). The will of God was that Jesus should die for the sake of human salvation as a ransom for human sins. One cannot say that Jesus had no faith based on the negative response to his prayer. Instead, he had a strong faith in God. He reached the extent of commending his soul into

---

[12] Christopher Dawson, *Progress and Religion: An historical enquiry into the Causes and Development of the Idea of Progress and its Relationship to Religion.* New York: Image Books, 1960, pp. 7-8.

the hands of God whom he claimed to have had forsaken him (Mathew 27:46). Later, God granted to Jesus what was more than not being tortured, and more than not dying. He was raised from the dead, the status which is beyond temporary successes as it encompasses eternity.

Again, with regard to recognizing human limitations and failures in life, eight years ago I met the Pentecostal pastor in the hospital who prayed for sick people, but at the end he forced miracles to happen but without success. He told one sick person that she would be discharged from the hospital after three days; the sick person said that she would be happy since she had been there for many days. Another sick person was told that she would be discharged after 7 days; the sick person responded by thanking him but complained as to why she had to stay more days than the other sick person.

Suddenly, he showed them an empty bed and told them that he had told the sick person who was on that bed that she would be discharged within few days to come, that is why she was not there anymore. The sick people told the pastor that the one who was on that bed was not discharged, but rather she had died early in the morning. This created shame on the pastor, who said with pain that may God give her eternal rest. When we pray we say, "thy will be done", not our will to be done, as we recognize our human limitations. When we pray, we cannot guarantee the outcome of our prayers. Prosperity cannot be guaranteed by human calculations.

Another example is Job, whose children, servants and livestock died. He became seriously sick, and was persuaded by his wife and friends to forsake God and die. But Job remained stable in faith despite all failures and sufferings. This shows that poor conditions are not signs of being forsaken by God. Job even contends that sometimes, wicked people do not have troubles, while righteous people have many troubles (Job 22). Job reaches the extent of saying that if good things come from God, even bad things can be expected from God (Job 2:10). This stance is related to divine determinism, which maintains that God determines all things, good and bad ones, to safeguard God's omnipotence, foreknowledge and pre-destination. Luther had the same opinion, that God is the source of all things, good and bad ones. For him, thinking that bad things do not come from God would lead to breaking the first commandment which forbids fearing other powers.[13] For Luther, when we are confronted by bad things, we are directed to depend on God, and hope for his promises that we get from Jesus Christ.[14] Challenges and difficulties in lives have made some African Christians change denominations severally in search of a prosperous life while blaming the previous denomination as weak and unable to bring about prosperity. God is with His people in times of joy and sorrows, in times of prosperity and poverty as they struggle towards better life

---

[13] Klaus Nürnberg, *Christi and the Ancestors in a changing Africa: The Living Dead and the Living God.* Pietermaritzburg: Cluster Publications, 2007, pp. 115-117.
[14] Ibid., p. 115.

conditions. God is with His people whether miracles are done or not, whether prayers are positively or negatively answered.

Although Jesus did miracles to address life's challenges for people's welfare, he sometimes hesitated to make miracles, and sometimes discouraged them to help his followers think beyond temporary successes, to include eternal dimensions in his ministry. When the disciples told him that the demons were submitting to them, Jesus told them that although they have been given power to make miracles and to overcome enemies, they should not to be happy because of that, they had to be happy because their names are written in heaven (Luke 10:17-20).

When people asked Jesus to make miracles by providing them with food, Jesus told them to seek food that does not perish, they have to seek eternal food (John 6:27). When Satan told Jesus to change stones into bread, Jesus rejected to do that miracle; he told Satan that humans should not live by bread alone, but also by the Word of God. Even when the Pharisees and Sadducees demanded miracles and signs from Jesus, Jesus told them that the cursed generation desires miracles; it will only see the signs of Jonah (Mathew 16:1-20) who was swallowed by a whale and later was vomited along the sea for refusing to obey God's instructions.

Relationship between Theology and Economics

Having seen the complexities of theologies of poverty and wealth, one of the solutions is to have a positive relationship between theology and economics. Church history shows that the church has been engaged in socio-economic life of people for many years. There was even a time when theology was viewed as a queen of science when universities started in the 12th century. But in the 18th century, modernism separated theology from public life, hence limiting the church's role of orienting the economic and social spheres of life. As a result, there was social exclusion of the poor, especially in the 19th century, following the negative effects of industrialization. Nevertheless, there were Christians who were committed to being advocates of the weak and to challenge social injustice.[15]

The need to relate the Christian faith to socio-economic life is echoed by the emergence of the home mission or modern *diakonia,* that emerged in the 19th century in Germany as a movement aimed at counteracting the social exclusion and disintegration caused by the industrial revolution. This home mission did its best to connect faith with efforts to eradicate socio-economic miseries,[16] not

---

[15] *Christian Faith and World Economy Today: A Study Document from the WCC.* Geneva: WCC, 1992, pp. 8-15.
[16] Alfred Jäger, *Diakonie als christliches Unternehmen: Theologische Wirtschaftsethik im KontextdiakonischerUnternehmenspolitik* 4 Auflage. Gütersloh: Gürtersloher Verlagshaus Gerd Mohn, 1993, pp. 55-57. Compare Matthias Benad, "Einleitung" in

only in Germany, but also in German colonies like Tanzania (then Tanganyika), where the Bethel Mission established hospitals, schools and agricultural training as a means of doing mission, and responded to the physical and spiritual needs of the people of Tanzania/German East Africa.[17] However, modern *diakonia*, was criticized by religious socialists for limiting itself to charitable work of helping the poor without contradicting the structures of exploitation, oppression and injustice.[18]

A Need for Positive Relationship between Theology and Economics so as to Combat Poverty

Economics, which mainly deals with the scientific analysis of production, distribution and consumption of goods and services, operates in the realm of power that is mainly used by the rich to undermine the poor and the weak. As such, economics necessarily involves value judgment and cannot be separated from theology and other fields of human life that guide and orientate economics in order to avoid oppression, exploitation, exclusion of the poor and the destruction of nature.[19] As Alfred Jäger observes, church and economy represent neither equal nor parallel interests. The concern about material survival on the one hand, and hope for a chance of getting a successful life from God while loving others on the other hand, is in permanent tension with each other.[20]

While theology and churches need economics to pursue their goals, economics also needs theology to orientate it for ethical purposes. The bridge

---

Matthias Benad (ed.) *Bethel Mission (1): Zwischen Epileptischenpflege und Heidenbekehrung: Beiträge zur Westfälischen Kirchengeschichte*, Band 19. Bielefeld: Luther Verlag, 2001, pp. ix-xv.

[17] Thorsten Altena, "Missionare und Einheimische Gesellschaft: Zur Kulturbegegnung der Bethel-Mission in Deutsch-Ostafrika 1890-1916." In Matthias Benad (ed.) *Bethel Mission (1)*, pp. 7-70. See also A. Danga Mndeme, "Gemeindediakonie." Diakonenschule Nazareth Fachseminar für Gemeindepflege, Bethel, 15 June, 1983, pp. 3-35. Also Niwagila, *From the Catacomb*, pp. 121-127, 215-226.

[18] Traugott Roser and Renatte Zitt, "Vom Monolog zum Dialog- von Sozialer Tat zu soziale Ordnung: zur Beziehung zwischen Theolgie und Oekonomie." In Dietzfelbinger (ed.), p. 39.

[19] *Christian Faith*, pp. 4-51. Compare Jäger, *Wirtschaftsethik als ökonomisches und christliches Postulat*, pp. 9-13. It has to be noted that before the emergence of the classical economy in the 18th century, economy was mainly concerned with the management of the household resources with regard to production, distribution, sharing and consumption of goods. The modern concept of economics as an academic subject that leads to analytical and professional competence, which is useful in finance, industry and government, goes back to Adam Smith, the Scottish moral philosopher who is known as "the father of economics" following the publication of his book, *The wealth of nations*, in 1776. *Christian Faith*, p. 5ff.

[20] Jaeger, *Wirtschaftsethik als Oekonomisches und Christlisches Postulat*, pp. 3-13.

between theology and economics is economic ethics, which brings together specialists from different fields such as economics, theology, philosophy and law, with a purpose of making sure that the pursuit of individual interests considers fairness in the market, humanity, social justice, competition, sustainability of economy, nature protection, satisfaction of employees, and co-operation with them.[21]

Thus, economic ethics is relevant in the whole process of combating poverty, and bringing about prosperity that is obtained without corruption, exploitation, dehumanization, and inequities. This indicates the positive relationship between theology and economics when both need each other. Otherwise, a negative relationship between the two may imply theology and churches which ignore economics that would benefit churches with their management of financial, human and material resources. The same applies to the advantages of economics to churches and Christians in the aspects of planning, implementation and the evaluation of church and individuals' activities.[22] A positive relationship between theology and economics demands constant dialogue between the two disciplines, so that theology and economics do not harm each other. When theologians will be equipped with knowledge about economics, they will have paved the way for a prophetic voice that advocates for the poor, and fights the structures that cause poverty.[23]

The negative relationship between theology and economics implies prayers without working while the one who instructed people to pray is the one who told them to seek, knock and struggle for success (Mt. 7:7). The relationship between theology and economics will encourage the stewardship of being responsible and accountable Christians before God by taking care of God's creation, keeping the Garden of Eden, and working upon it without destroying it. The same applies to acquiring wealth justifiably without exploiting others, while having the diaconal spirit of assisting the needy like orphans, widows and those who have physical challenges.

The relationship between theology and economics enables the church to prepare Christians in the aspects of entrepreneurship, so that they can be able to create wealth by undertaking small or big businesses. The same applies to the church's engagement in micro-finance credit societies, which have helped the poor to access finances for their small projects of agriculture and small businesses. Such micro-finance credit societies have helped many people to get money for schools fees, medical care, and house construction. Paul's self-reliance by making tents for supporting church ministry (2 Thes. 3:10) is a source of encouraging church leaders and congregants to make and acquire wealth for their successful life and betterment of church ministry, without being derailed from the biblical truth by prosperity gospel preachers.

---

[21] Ibid., pp. 3-13.
[22] Keshomshahara, *A Theology of Poverty Reduction*, p. 256.
[23] Ibid., pp. 209- 210.

Such initiatives for self-reliance and the creation of wealth should be supported by churches as an alternative right way that quenches the thirst of being prosperous. The same applies to church organizations which can create wealth by putting in place income-generating projects like rental houses, hotels, forests, and agricultural activities. Such projects can help the church to pursue its goals of evangelization, *diakonia*, advocacy and offering social services like education and health.

The church ought to offer its services in view of the Bible and the application of economic techniques. We ought to know well the services we offer in the church and give them a value. People are waiting to receive the church services of Holy Communion, burial services, counselling, visitations, sermons, prayers, songs, and the presence of Christians and pastors in several social religious events. People are eager to receive church services like Christian education, seminars, secular education, health services, hotel services, and rental houses. After knowing the services we offer, we ought to ask ourselves if we make these services available to the people. We should not just end up with making them available to the people, but also ask ourselves if we offer those services in a way that is attractive, not boring, and if the services we offer are of quality.

Do we use technology to communicate with our people? We have churches with big buildings without the media for making the sermon heard. This is where we have good food on a bad plate. In Judah 1:3-4, the Bible challenges the Christians to vigorously defend and contend for the beliefs that we cherish against the false prophets who are misleading people. This text challenges us to struggle and compete like business people for the sake of the biblical truth.

When it comes to fundraising for certain projects, we are supposed to consider giving feedback to the contributors for the sake of transparency, and encouraging them to give more in supporting church projects. All these are biblical and economic principles for openness, transparency and accountability since such income does not belong to the individual but to the church. The same discipline and principles are needed for individual and corporate businesses.

Conclusion

A positive relationship between theology and economics is one of the ways that addresses theological and economic issues that trouble member churches in Africa as far as the complexities of theologies of poverty, wealth and prosperity are concerned. There is a need of combating poverty without falling into the danger of spiritualizing material poverty, or glorifying wealth as if wealth is a precondition or a sign of having faith, or being predestined to eternal life.

Theology and churches need economics with its techniques of management of financial, human and material resources for the sustainability of church work. Economic principles will help Christians and churches to work hard and produce more, as they pursue diaconal love of the neighbour while depending on God without being inactive. It has to be noted that prayers should not replace seeking and knocking; also working hard should not replace prayers. When the church appreciates and applies economic principles in the creation of wealth, it will be able to empower Christians with entrepreneurship for small and big businesses. Even the church will be able to create wealth that is needed to pursue evangelization, *diakonia*, advocacy, and the provision of social services in the society to bear Christian witness in words and deeds.

Furthermore, economics needs theology as a source of ethical orientation against exploitation, oppression, cruelty, brutality and the exclusion of the poor. Thus, economic ethics bridges the gap between theology and economics. When economics is oriented by theology and ethics, then peace will prevail in societies and the world at large. The role of churches in the cancellation of debts for poor countries in the year 2000 proves the role of theology in economics. The cancellation of debts enabled the poor to access social services, since money that would have paid debts was earmarked for social services. This led to poverty reduction in the countries that benefited from debt cancellation.

Churches in Africa ought to apply business principles in offering her services to the people. This goes hand in hand with the need for customer care of the Christians and the entire community. There is a need of making our services known to the people with a clear timetable showing the place and time of the service to be offered. Transparency, openness and accountability are needed when it comes to fundraising and the use of money. Reporting to the Christians who raise funds for the church is necessary, different from churches which use church income as if it is meant for an individual church leader or a small group of people. Thus, the positive relationship between theology and economics will make churches in Africa sustainable in pursuit of their goals. It will even make economics meaningful to the people whom it aims to serve.

A Theological Response to the Ecological Crisis, Wealth and Prosperity
Frouisou Samuel

Human beings are created in the image of God (the Creator); they are an integral part of the divine creation. As beings created in the likeness of God, humans have received from their Creator the responsibility of preserving and caring for the creation, cf. Genesis chapter 1, verses 26-31.[1] Nowadays, the problem of "ecological crisis and theological challenges of wealth and prosperity" is pertinent because there is a threat to the survival of the human species, a threat caused by evils like environmental degradation, pollution, desertification and selfishness of so-called developed nations. In this sense, reflecting on "ecological crisis and theological challenges of wealth and prosperity", in the present African context, is nothing but tackling the important question of stewardship and accountability to God, in the management of material, financial, and spiritual resources, for the common good of God's entire creation.

What is an "ecological crisis"? What are theological and convictional challenges linked to the problem of wealth and prosperity, today? How can we address the current ecological crisis and theological challenges of wealth and prosperity in the African context? Nowadays, to address the ecological crisis as a place and a chance for a theological challenge of wealth and prosperity is nothing but recognizing the plurality of theological convictions on the issues of stewardship and accountability to God. In other words, when we talk about human responsibility in the destruction of the creation by ills such as desertification, pollution, drought, recurrent floods and global warming, among others, for example, we do not always share the same social, economic, political and religious convictions, depending on whether we are from the side of so-called developed countries of the West, or on the side of developing countries like Africa.

Therefore, this article bases itself on economic and religious convictions, in order to deal with theological challenges of wealth and prosperity in post-modern societies, with a particular focus on living the realities of creation by following the biblical, ascetic, and sacramental models of creation.

---

[1] *La Bible*, Edition bilingue, Français et Anglais. Nairobi: Alliance Biblique Universelle, 2010, p. 3.

In a globalized world, sometimes called a 'global village', it is easy to think that everyone should conform to the prevailing culture. In this regard, those who do not conform or who resist one or the other of the dominant cultures are treated as "barbarians", or, "uncivilized". In this sense, African societies, as a whole, are also faced with the challenges of adapting their political, economic, socio-cultural and religious systems of organization to the new world order, and, if not, they simply disappear. This is why, in most African countries, there is nowadays a great confusion as to the actions to be taken, faced with "the ecological crisis and the theological challenge of wealth and prosperity", which is shaking up this world called a 'global village'.

In other words, the problem of the "ecological crisis and the theological challenge of wealth and prosperity" lies at the centre of debates affecting as deeply as well as completely the integrity of human life, in relation to the environment in which we live, both materially, morally and spiritually. More than in the past, the question of the ecological crisis and that of the theological challenge linked to the polysemic concepts of 'wealth' and 'prosperity', from an existential perspective, arises with acuity because there is a real and certain threat to the survival of the human species. The consequences of such a crisis, we can well imagine, very negatively affect African societies that are still lagging behind because they are unbalanced by both endogenous and exogenous forces.

It is here that it should also be remembered, and strongly denounce the fact that it was intentionally that the dominant civilizations of Judeo-Christian and Arab-Muslim origin, set up systems of exploitation of natural resources, during periods of historical encounters between the different peoples of the earth, in order to ensure the well-being of human beings, both temporally and spiritually. But the results of such enterprises, as we now know, are recurring evils, from which the whole of humanity suffers. They are, among others, evils such as environmental degradation, pollution, desertification, climate change, famine, and the problem of the availability and judicious distribution of arable land. These evils are closely linked to the issue of sustainable development, a subject of a declaration adopted by the United Nations General Assembly in September 2015.[2]

Faced with this burning issue, that is to say, faced with the impact and effects of the ecological crisis and the theological challenge of wealth and prosperity, in an African context, what can or what should be the contribution of African Christian Churches, members of the All Africa Conference of Churches (AACC)? The main objective of this communication is to underline the importance of community life, the expression of solidarity, in the African

---

[2] At the heart of the 2030 agenda, 17 Sustainable Development Goals (SDGs) were set in September 2015. They cover all of the development issues in all countries such as climate, bio-diversity, energy, water, poverty, gender equality, economic prosperity, peace, agriculture, and education.

context, on the one hand, and of the evaluation, from a historical perspective, of the effects of the different encounters between the civilizations of Non-African origin and African cultures, on the black continent, on the other hand. Because in Africa, we do not speak of "wealth", let alone of "prosperity", outside of community life. The African concept of *Ubuntu* excludes any individualism, any egoism, and any exploitation of nature and / or of the human being, created by God, and whose life is sacred, for mercantilist purposes. In other words, in the African context, the notions of 'wealth' and 'prosperity' have very different meanings from those given to them by the advocates of unconditional globalization.

More precisely, and to respond to this concern relating to the sub-theme of: "the ecological crisis and the theological challenge of wealth and prosperity, in Africa", we will first present the three conceptions of the world as an attempt to explain the biblical advent of a new heaven and a new earth (according to the Book of Revelation, chapter 21, verses 1-5); then present the current context of the ecological crisis and the theological challenge of wealth and prosperity in Africa; to finally define the contribution of the Christian Churches of Africa, in order to meet this challenge of the ecological crisis in a perspective of the theology of 'wealth' and 'prosperity', in vogue today.

Biblical Conceptions of a New Heaven and a New Earth (Rev.21: 1-5)

What do we mean by the term "ecological crisis"? What are the theological and convictional challenges related to the theological challenges of 'wealth' and 'prosperity' in Africa today? How can we approach the question of this 'ecological crisis', within the framework of an inter-convictional theological dialogue, capable of bringing together and integrating human beings in their physical and spiritual environments, so that, whatever the convictions or the religious, philosophical, political and economic faiths, which guide their actions, vis-à-vis nature, we can respond, in a responsible way, to the imminent threat of this 'ecological crisis' which weighs on all of humanity? These are, among other concerns, some of the questions that will guide our thinking in this first part of our presentation.

First of all, talking about the 'ecological crisis' as a place and opportunity for a theological and inter-convictional dialogue, nowadays, is to automatically recognize the plurality of theological convictions on this question whose importance is no longer to be demonstrated. In other words, when we approach the question of human responsibility in this ecological crisis, the consequences of which are, among others, desertification, pollution, drought, recurrent floods and global warming, having immediate impacts on the lives of human beings, it is very difficult to share the same convictions, everywhere and in all human societies.

Given the reality of the harmful effects of this ecological crisis on the environment, no one should, therefore, be indifferent, whatever their political, economic, ideological or religious convictions, in the face of the threat to planet earth, 'the *ecumene*', which is our common living space. In the same vein, we propose to integrate, or initiate, a theological and inter-convictional dialogue, with a view to achieving just, reliable and beneficial results for all. Hence, the need to build a constructive and inclusive reflection around the following three ways of conceiving and living, with intelligence and love, the realities of divine creation, our common home: it is a question of dealing with an iconographic vision (icon, or image), liturgy (celebration, artistic beauty) and asceticism of the world created by God, and to bring out the three biblical models closely linked to life on earth, in accordance with the human responsibility to take care of it.

How can mankind reverse the process of corruption and pollution of the physical environment, which seems to be irreversible nowadays? How should human beings deal with the multidimensional damage their actions are causing to planet earth, our common home? And how can or should human beings act in accordance with the vision, or the creationist account of the book of Genesis? The convictions based on the accounts of the revealed religions of Abrahamic origin, namely, Judaism, Christianity and Islam, present three avenues of research, with a view to the restoration, *"Tikkun Olam"*[3] of the earth, which groans under the destructive effect of the combined action of sin and greed in human beings (see Hosea 4:3 and Rom 8:22).

The Iconographic Vision of the World as a
Possible Solution for the Restoration of Creation

An icon is defined as a way of perceiving, understanding and representing the elements of nature in their interactions. It is, in fact, the conception whereby every element created by God, every element that has the breath of life in it, is holy (see Psalm 150: 6). In other words, when our heart is sensitive to this reality of things, our eyes open to clearly discern the beauty of created things, according to Abba Isaac the Syrian.[4]

---

[3] In the teaching of Judaism, *Tikkun Olam* recalls any activity aimed at improving the harmonious state of the original creation. *Tikkun Olam* also means that the world was created good; its Creator intentionally provided an opportunity to improve the state of His work. Also, all human activities should be considered as opportunities to accomplish this mission. As such, any person, regardless of their social status, can and should be associated with *Tikkun Olam*: child or adult, student or entrepreneur, industrialist or artist, social worker or merchant, political activist or environmentalist, or any other person here among us, who fights against the deterioration of creation, in view of its restoration.

[4] Le Syrien, A. I., *Light through Darkness: Orthodox Spirituality.* Maryknoll, NY: Orbis Books, 2004.

Icons restore and reconcile, they remind us that we are not the only creatures of God living in the cosmos; they offer us possibilities to correct our destructive cultures of our environment. Icons reveal to us what the values of all of God's creatures really are, and why God created them. Icons engage us, or rather engage our theological convictions in a perspective of faith in the advent, or in the realization of the Kingdom of heaven on earth. They (the icons) help us distance ourselves from philosophical considerations which differentiate matter from the spiritual, the temporal from the eternal, and the created from the uncreated.

This is why, in the Christian religion, for example, the doctrine of the incarnation is at the heart of iconography (see Psalm 45:2; John 1:1, 18; Rom.8:18-22). In this sense, the whole creation is an icon. Because "nothing is for nothing before God," Irenaeus[5] would say. This is why in the icons, the rivers have a human form, as well as the sun, the moon and the stars that God created (see Psalm 8:4-8).

The Liturgical Vision of Creation

When we consider the actions of human beings on their physical environment, we are far from realizing that these actions are damaging to the eco-system on which all life on earth depends for preservation. In their daily actions, human beings behave like simple tourists, extra-terrestrials whose survival would be totally independent of that of the earth, from which they nevertheless draw all the resources necessary for their existence. Taking a closer look, human actions on the environment carry in themselves the germ of original sin, that is to say, of the pride and disobedience of the human being, instead of the responsibility of the latter, vis-à-vis the creation of God, as defined in the book of Genesis, chapters 1 and 2.[6]

The liturgy is precisely an exaltation of the communion between God, the peoples and the other things which God has created. For it is through the liturgy that God is celebrated in His creation, as well as by humans, trees, birds, stars, and the moon (see Psalm 19:1). Thus, if we forget that our life is a liturgy which consists in imploring God for the renewal of our cosmos polluted by our irresponsible actions, we are far from being those creatures that God made a little inferior to himself.

---

[5] Irenaeus lived in the 2nd century, and wrote a number of books, the most important of which is: *Contre les hérésies dénonciation et réfutation de la gnose au nom menteur*, traduit par le Moine Adelin Rousseau. Amazon Books, 2001.
[6] *La Bible.* Edition bilingue, Français et Anglais. Nairobi: Alliance Biblique Universelle, 2010, pp. 1-4.

The Ascetic Vision of the World as a Solution to the Environmental Crisis

Asceticism should not always be understood as contempt, the flight from matter for the benefit of the spiritual. Lynn White, in an article entitled, "The Roots of our Ecological Crisis," notes the following: "The Eastern Saint Contemplates; the Saint of the West acts; the Latins thought that sin was moral evil, and that salvation should be found in good behaviour...the implications of Christianity in the conquest of nature should, therefore, come more easily from the West" (Science 155, March 1967, pp. 1203-07"). It appears, according to this author, that a contemplative vision of nature by man is more sober and gentle, in terms of the impact on creation, than an aggressive action. Therefore, to have an ascetic view of the world in order to solve the problems of ecological crisis, is to learn to offer, to share and to reconnect, at the same time, with one's fellow human beings and with nature. It is also to move away from our selfishness and to love other creatures through the love of God, the Creator.

If our ecological commitments must leave the field of theoretical and convictional dissensions, to take shape in concrete actions, we will have to follow the three models mentioned below, models which are moreover complementary, in our search for solutions to environmental problems; these include the biblical model, the ascetic model, and the sacramental model.

According to the ascetic model, the solution to the ecological crisis could come from putting into practice the three letters R, namely, Renunciation, Repentance and Responsibility.

- Renunciation consists in using material goods with parsimony and intelligence. It is about living simply, and simply live.
- Repentance: through repentance, we must confess, and confess that we have abused of the land, and by doing so, we have failed in our vocation to cultivate and keep the land (see Genesis 2: 15).
- Responsibility: our responsibility is engaged in the way in which we respond to "the call of God", in the face of the challenge of preserving his creation. We are called to surrender to the wisdom and love of God who wants us to be responsible for the renewal of his creation, according to Rev.21 and Rom. 8.

Thus, one of the major challenges to be taken up by the Christian Churches in Africa lies in taking into consideration the word of Jesus: "give them food yourselves" (Mt. 14: 16b), and putting into practice this other saying: "Give us this day our daily bread" (Mt. 6:11).

Meeting the challenges of sustainable development, in the current context, will mean dealing, among other things and this from a theological and pastoral perspective, with the issue of climate change, food security and the management of creation. Hence the following question: How do we train men and women, capable of giving their best for the cause of the poor, the hungry and those left behind in the "global village"? What are the tools or arguments that African Christians need, which can enable them to "feed themselves", and ask God for the "daily bread" for those in need?

In other words, our concern in this second part of this presentation deals with the theological and pastoral approach of the words of Jesus: "give them something to eat yourselves" and of: "when you pray say: "Give us this day our daily bread".

Current Ecological Crisis and the Theological Challenge of Wealth and Prosperity in Africa

During the meeting of the Association of Theological Training Institutions in Francophone Africa, bringing together the theological institutes affiliated to AACC, from Benin, Burundi, Cameroon, Central African Republic (CAR), Congo-Brazzaville, Cote d'Ivoire, Gabon, Rwanda and Togo (ASTHEOL), held in Yaoundé, from December 13 to 15, 2016, the heads of these institutions, together with their partners in the church's mission in Africa, looked at the very evocative theme of: "Keeping the flame alive: the churches of Africa in the face of today's major challenges". The presentations, very varied and rich in their content, focused on sub-themes ranging from "the radicalization of religions and the instability of states in Africa, to "the family in Africa at a time of socio-political change", through "traditional churches and new forms of beliefs", "climate change, food security and the land issue", and, "churches in the face of the tragedies of migration and disease". At the end of this meeting in Yaoundé, one of the strong resolutions was to "train the workers of the churches of Africa so that they are informed people, capable of meeting the challenges of the day which African Christian churches are facing".

In a report published by the Nagel Institute of Calvin College, in June 2014, on the theme of "Engaging African Realities", African leaders, including ministers of worship, university lecturers, theologians, philosophers, researchers in social sciences and natural sciences, have committed the churches to train men and women capable of addressing the current challenges of sustainable development.[7]

After more than half a century of autonomy of the Christian churches in Africa, most of their theological and pastoral training seminars, for example, continue to operate on the basis of Christian doctrines and practices, established by the founding missionary societies. Training in these theological institutes and faculties is carried out as if they were training people to meet the needs of men and women of the nineteenth-century.[8] This should no longer be

---

[7] Joel Carpenter and Nellie Kooistra, "Engaging Africa: Report", New York: Nagel Institute for the Study of World Christianity, Nagel Institute of Calvin College, 2014.
[8] In the 19th century, the "Religious Awakening" crossed all of Europe. The Protestant Revival and Catholic Renewal constitute the most proselytizing forms of Western

the case because as C. Peter Wagner acknowledges, "Seminaries previously functioned like dental schools or police academies. The job market is closed to those who haven't been to the approved schools. When this was the case, seminaries had an established constituency, and they could function almost indefinitely. No longer."[9] Thus, given the new context, theological and pastoral training institutes in Africa, must adapt to the new situation[10] in order to meet the current challenges of humanity threatened by multidimensional crises.

In order that our Christian Churches in Africa can respond to the new challenges of humanity, we must ensure that the curricula place more emphasis on the training of leaders or practitioners of sustainable development, who are committed to improving the conditions of life of the members of their faith communities, than on the production of academicians concerned with old confessional doctrines, elaborated by the missionary societies, to meet the needs of the emerging Christian communities in the 'mission lands' of that time. Because, according to John Leith, describing the situation which currently prevails in the institutions of theological and pastoral training of the traditional or historical churches, resulting from these missionary societies of Western origin: "Several basic Christian doctrines are in danger on the campuses of seminaries nowadays. There is little evidence of a passion for proclaiming fundamental Christian convictions of the faith, or of the Christian message announcing the good news of God's salvation for all humans."[11] This situation of all-out crisis that our African churches are going through has the

---

Christianity. Groups praying for missionaries sent to the world by mission societies, notably the London Mission (LMS) founded in 1795 and the Basel Mission founded in 1815, multiplied. Baptists, Reformed, Lutherans, Independents come together for the mission. But in the field of the mission, misunderstandings emerged, and quickly, we witnessed the establishment of biblical and pastoral training structures, in accordance with the particular doctrines of the missionary churches. Here, special emphasis is placed on the spiritual formation of local personnel; over there, it is a workforce in the service of the "missionary-trader-settler" that preoccupies those responsible for the formation. See also the excellent articles by Joseph KIizerbo, "The influence of Western cultural models on African societies", and by Miche Sauvetre, "Des Ecoles, Pourquoi faire?", In Flambeau Spécial Education, Nos. 34-35, May-August, 1972, pp. 95-108 and 111-127.
[9] C. Peter Wagner, *Churchquake!* Ventura, CA, Regal Books, 1999, p. 223.
[10] In a context of multidimensional crisis where voices are being raised increasingly in favour of a holistic training of pastors, theologians and social workers, it becomes more than urgent for the theological and pastoral training to include in its curricula, in addition to the purely spiritual teachings, subjects such as: 'Study of the natural environment', 'Population growth', 'Environmental management', 'Technology and environment'. See also the excellent works by Joe Holland and Peter Henriot, SJ, *Social Analysis: Linking Faith and Justice*, Maryknoll, NY: Orbis Books, 1984, and by James Cochrane, John de Cruchy and Robin Petersen, *In Word and Deed, Towards A Practical Theology for Social Transformation.* Pietermaritzburg: Cluster Publications, 1991.
[11] John H. Leith, *Crisis in the Church: The Plight of Theological Education*, Louisville, KY: Westminster John Knox, 1997, p. 10.

immediate consequence "that theological seminaries are no longer considered above all as institutes for the training of pastors, but as places of discussion and the study of religion".[12]

Therefore, the curricula in these theological and pastoral training institutes are made up of more than 80% of theories, and less than 20% of practices. Hence, the often inappropriate nature of the lessons given in these seminaries, which for the most part are inadequate to train men and women capable of meeting the current challenges of sustainable development in Africa and in the world. It is in this sense that the Dean, Michael Bame Bame, in his closing speech of the Interdisciplinary Week of the 1987/1988 academic year, on the theme: "The Church and Education", deplored the situation: "We note with great regret that the education system adopted by most of our countries only promotes human development on two levels: intellectual and psychomotor, to the detriment of the other two. This education system, which underlies the materialistic ideology, seems arbitrary and dangerous to us, especially for Africa, because it undermines the heritage of the black man, that is, his all-encompassing vision of reality and of life. We encourage our governments to get rid of any materialistic ideology imported from the West in the field of education, which deprives man and society of his conscience and his soul."[13]

In 2007, the communion of Lutheran churches, united within the Lutheran World Federation[14] (LWF), through its development and mission department, produced a documentary dealing with the theme entitled: "Together to heal the world; 60 years of common worldwide diaconia". This documentary reviews six decades of activities carried out by the LWF, as a communion of churches, in fields as varied as those of reconciliation, the promotion of justice, peace and solidarity between peoples torn by various conflicts, the contribution to economic recovery, and the encouragement of the participation of local communities in the processes of holistic development.

As part of the celebration of the five hundred years of the Protestant Reformation of the sixteenth century, which is an integral part of the 7th decade (2007-2017) of the LWF, we are also struck by the recurrence of the themes selected, such as: render justice to the poor and the oppressed, the problem of food, the question of health, of reconciliation, and the problem of water. All these efforts have been pursued during many long years of activities of Christian witness in the world, despite all the material and human means mobilized by this communion of churches since 1947, in order to help the poor of our planet.

---

[12] Ibid.
[13] Collection Semaine Interdisciplinaire Année Académique 1987/1988 sur le thème de: 'L'Eglise et l'Education', Faculté de Théologie Protestante de Yaoundé.
[14] LWF was created in 1947, to deal with the reconstruction of the world after the Second World War.

In this sense, the words of Jesus: "give them food yourselves." (Mt. 14: 16b), and when you pray say, "Give us this day our daily bread" (Mt. 6:11), become a pressing challenge for our churches in Africa, which are going through generalized crises, of both internal and external origin. But in fact, as disciples and envoys of Christ, as Church leaders who face these multidimensional challenges, what can or should be our theological and pastoral contribution? What do we have to offer our communities, and more especially, those among us who are threatened in their physical existence, as a result of this ecological crisis? How do we feed those who lack food and ask for it today? What does it really mean to pray for 'daily bread' today?

The Role of Prayer in Managing Ecological Crisis

Praying for a daily bread means meeting the current challenges of climate change, food security and the problem of the earth: "Prayer is risky; it commits the one who prays to follow it up with a corresponding action."[15] In as much as: "The problems of hunger in the world are so overwhelming that we are tempted to think, like the disciples: 'Send them away', or, as the rich man: 'Send Lazarus beyond the grave to warn my brothers."[16] Knowing the answer that Jesus gave to these two concerns, "Give them food yourselves", and, "Your brothers have prophets and preachers with them on earth, let them listen to them", we should emphasize prayer in our institutions of theological and pastoral training.

In the Bible, it is not only verse 11 of Matthew 6 or verse 3 of Luke 11, its parallel, quoted above, which deal with the prayer for "daily bread". We can also draw inspiration from the books of Gen. 28: 20-22; Prov. 30: 8-9; Ex. 16: 1-17; and 1Kgs. 17: 8-16, to encourage our learners to take their prayer life seriously. Like the examples of prayers formulated in these passages, by men of God to ask Him for food for their own material needs and for those of the people for whom they are responsible: it concerns their needs to eat, drink, protect themselves against heat or cold, and against diseases which destroy the biological or physical balance of God's creatures.

For this reason, as teachers of theology and pastors of churches of the Protestant Reformation of the sixteenth century, we cannot help but rediscover with the potential readers of this presentation, the explanations that one of the great Reformers of the Christian Church, in this case, Dr. Martin Luther, gave of the 4th request of the "Lord's Prayer", in his Small Catechism.[17]

---

[15] "To all of you." In *Give Us Today Our Daily Bread*, Eleventh General Assembly of the LWF, Study Materials, Day Two, 2007, p. 7.
[16] Ibid., p. 7.
[17] *La foi des Eglises luthériennes: Confessions et catéchismes*, Textes édités par André Birmelé et Marc Lienhard. Paris: Editions du Cerf, 1991, p. 309.

According to Martin Luther, "God gives bread to all men, even to the wicked, and this regardless of our prayer".[18] But, in this prayer, he added, we ask that God give us a grateful heart, so that we can receive our daily bread with thanksgiving. When asked what is meant by the expression 'daily bread' contained in the 4th request of the Lord's Prayer, Luther said that it is about "all that is necessary for the maintenance of the body and of life, food and clothing, home, fields, cattle, money and all goods, a good husband, good children, faithful servants, just supervisors, good government, favourable seasons, peace, health, order, honour, good friends, friendly neighbours".[19]

This petition comes right in the middle of a series of seven requests. It should also be noted that of the seven requests, it is the only one which is concerned with the material needs of mankind. It is, therefore, quite clear that in the Lord's Prayer, emphasis is placed more on spiritual blessings than on material ones (six of the seven requests made are in favour of spiritual needs). But, in our prayers, we often reverse the order. Six of the seven requests we make to the Lord are generally for temporal needs. Is this not the preoccupation with wanting to own the material riches of this world at all costs that often leads us to selfishness: everything for me and nothing for others? Is this not this desire to accumulate material wealth for ourselves that makes us actors in the destruction of our own natural environment?

We should only eat our share of bread, not our own share, and that of others that the system has helped us take away from them. But unfortunately, "the problem of the 'haves' and' have-nots' is deeply 'rooted in the socio-economic system itself, of which, we are all a part",[20] and which is not easy to address without recourse to the Word of God.

In terms of a purely economic development, it is important to remember that relations between Africa and the outside world were essentially characterized by what Jean Yves Carfantan[21] and Charles Condamines called "aid that makes you hungry". It is no secret that the exclusive system of commerce between the metropolis and the colony, also known as the "colonial pact", consisted essentially of the development of the colony for the sole benefit of the metropolis.

When Westerners arrived in Africa, their primary objective was to exploit the resources that abound in Africa for economic needs. Thus, to maximize the use of arable land, it was a question of reviewing the traditional African agricultural production system, of introducing the so-called cash crops, of disorganizing the exchange systems based on barter, and to replace them with a

---

[18] Ibid., p. 309.
[19] Ibid., p. 309.
[20] «A toutes et à tous.» In Donne-nous aujourd'hui notre pain quotidien. Onzième Assemblée Générale de la FLM, Matériel d'Etude, Deuxième jour, 2007, p. 7.
[21] Carfantan, J. Y., *Vaincre la faim, c'est possible*, Paris: Seuil, 1983.

system essentially monetary and mercantile, for the benefit of the metropolis alone.

The introduction of currency, money, also called Mammon in biblical language, in the colonial economy, favoured the imbalance of the mechanisms of production and distribution of goods in African societies because, according to Jean Marc Ela, money "carries with it the crisis of traditional socio-economic balances".[22]

In order to better understand the drama that African peoples are living today, it must be noted that since we have been made to believe that having a lot of money in the bank is the real sign of wealth, of social success, and that human essence depends on what he owns, everyone fights hard for money and always a lot of money. But for what results, in the end? Are the budgets of African nations, which increase year after year, synonymous with the economic growth of these nations, which moreover are always described as underdeveloped? If so, why is Africa experiencing a food crises when at the same time it is recognized as one of the continents potentially rich in arable land?

In a survey carried out by Jean Yves Carfantan and Charles Condamines on the causes of hunger in Third World countries, including African countries, the French, in their overwhelming majority, attribute the causes of hunger in the Third World to bad governance: "They are hungry because they are badly governed and incapable of living in a democracy".[23] But if we follow the current debates on the issue of bad governance and the poverty of the African populations, the current givers of lessons in democracy and governance are not exempt from criticism.

The Pastoral Dimension of Prayer for 'Daily Bread' in the Churches of Africa

The responsibility of the church in the management of material, financial and spiritual resources in Africa, and in the world, is no longer to be demonstrated today. As spiritual guides and dispensers of divine grace to the people of God, pastors are, above all, men and women of prayer. The time they spend with God in intercession on behalf of His people makes them increasingly aware of the harsh realities of human life in this world. By devoting himself to the activity of prayer, the pastor has a deeper understanding of the struggle that Christians lead to meet their daily needs, both spiritual and material. Prayer makes us aware not only of the needs of others, but also of our own needs. In this sense, we pray the 'Lord's Prayer', not only when we are together for a worship celebration where we recite this model prayer, but also and above all, when we formulate specific prayers in favour of the poor who live among us. The pastor, and the Christian community which he leads pray to ensure that all

---

[22] J. M. Ela, *L'Afrique des villages*, Paris: Karthala, 1982, p. 13.
[23] Carfantan J. Y., op. cit., pp. 5-6.

the poor and hungry will receive what they need to nourish their bodies, and that together we will be satisfied both materially and spiritually.[24]

In the theological and pastoral training programmes of theological institutes, it should above all not be forgotten that, through the pastor, it is the church as a whole which also prays for the "bread of life". Jesus, the bread of life gives himself to his people, through the bread and wine of the Last Supper presided over by the pastor, minister of the Word and of the sacraments. The passages which deal with the theme of 'Christ the bread of life', without being explicitly formulated in the form of a prayer, are moreover very numerous in the Bible, the Word of God and the basis of all theological and pastoral teaching in our institutes and faculties of Protestant theology. We can cite as examples the passages in John 6: 1-11, where Jesus feeds five thousand men; John 6: 25-40, where he presents himself as the "bread of life"; and John 10: 7-16, which tells the story of the hireling who works for his belly, and of the good shepherd who leads the sheep into the green pasture and gives his life for them.

In explaining the Lord's Prayer to the faithful, pastors should draw the attention of the latter to the important aspects of this prayer, aspects which relate to the question of the availability of 'bread', and its equitable distribution to members of the community. The Seventh Commandment that says, "Thou shall not steal", also has important implications for the distribution of material wealth in the world today. We must not forget that from its beginnings, the church has always cared for the poor and the disinherited, working for a certain social revolution. According to Acts 4:32: "No one claimed that any of their possessions was their own, but they shared everything they had".

In the history of the Christian church, the fundamental question of the sound stewardship of the means with which God blesses humanity and that of the responsibility of those who play a leadership role within these communities was of great concern to everyone. The question of property and material possessions was at the heart of the debate over the role the Church should play in the social, political and economic spheres. Inspired by the narratives of Genesis 1:26 and Genesis 2:15, Popes Francis and Bonaventure developed the concepts of "stewardship without property", to address the problem of corruption and mismanagement of property of the church in the 13th century. In this same perspective, the Protestant Reformation of the 16th century has revived it, by reinterpreting the biblical notion of "vocation", in order to

---

[24] To be "materially full presupposes concrete actions aimed at producing material goods such as food, drink, clothing and shelter from the effects of weather". But, for Jesus, the Creator is already taking care of it. In other words, the prayer of the Christian must always precede the actions and not the contrary (Mt. 6: 25-34). If in this article, we focus on the concept of prayer, it is precisely to explain the importance of this activity (prayer is a priority activity in the life of believers), in relation to the concrete actions that Christians must lead for their testimony in the world.

revalue human work as a divine call through which each one exercises his talent for the well-being of all.

But, if the pastoral ministry can, and in some instances must, take on a diaconal dimension, the pastor sometimes being considered as a servant in the church or, even, as a servant of the church, what can be the concrete and practical implications of the exercise of his ministry over the life of the members of the church, and of the society in which he exercises this ministry?

Practical Dimension of 'Give Us Our Daily Bread' and the Realities of the Exercise of Pastoral Ministry in Africa

Is the pastor a servant in the church, or is he rather a servant of the church? Like Christ, his Master, the pastor should avoid being served or to be served to the detriment of others. It should be noted, however, that the temptation for pastors to seek service is often very great, despite many scriptural warnings against them (see 1 Peter 5: 1-4).

It is true that in most cases of abuse of authority or mismanagement noted among pastors, it is often found that they are driven by bad management structures, resulting from organizational systems that do not promote sharing, solidarity, and collegiality, while the pastoral ministry, as defined in the Holy Scriptures, is a collegial ministry. From then on, it becomes easy, but not normal, to understand that in our so-called traditional churches, pastors are cited as serving selfish and partisan interests, to the detriment of the interests of the whole church, and especially of the weakest among us. It is often difficult to accept the image that people have of the pastor in these churches, which have emerged from Western missionary societies. In most of these churches, the pastor is often seen as that person who does not hesitate to use Christians to achieve non-evangelical goals. But if the church wants the pastor to fully play his role of servant of the community, it would also be necessary to accept that he is a servant in this same community, that is to say, he must be given the necessary means of service that is required of him. If not, how can the pastor meet the needs of all with the sometimes very limited means at his disposal?

Far from being an excuse for pastors and those responsible for the management of the structures of religious institutions, through this questioning, is to encourage pastors to become aware of this practical and concrete dimension of their ministry, which consists in giving bread to eat, to those who are hungry. They are, moreover, very many in our society today who expect the pastor to give them this 'daily bread'. We would be surprised by this growing expectation of society, vis-à-vis pastors and other religious leaders, if rampant materialism and egoism had not ended up reducing human beings to their purely animal dimension, since in the traditional churches, the pastor has often been presented as that person, who is materially but also intellectually poor, who has no right to anything, especially to material possessions that have long been considered enemies of spiritual life. This is why, in our Christian communities, at least in the Protestant churches that emerged from Western missionary societies, the pastors, trained in theological seminaries, think that the needs of the faithful for whom they are responsible, were first and foremost, spiritual. But with the reality of the 4th request of the "Lord's Prayer", we understand that these needs can also and are even firstly, material. Yet in either case, the pastor in our context today cannot claim to be able to respond favourably to the needs of all at once and at the same time. This is why he must use all the material and human means at his disposal in his community to respond to the requests of the faithful, in relying on his training received during biblical and theological training seminars.

In our struggle to give 'bread' to all, we must not forget that the Lord himself has promised to bless his church with all the necessary gifts that we need to function as a community of brothers and sisters, sharing all in common, according to 1 Cor. 12: 18-27.

Conclusion

This article highlighted the role and importance of the teaching and practice of theology as a determining factor for sustainable and harmonious development in the African context today. The profound changes that we are witnessing in Africa today affect all walks of life. But the religious or spiritual aspect seems to be the most important. While it is not true to say that African culture is primarily spiritual, whereas that of the West is primarily materialistic,[25] a distinction can be made between the two ways of seeing the world.

The universe, according to an African, is a field of forces in perpetual dialectical interaction in search of new balances. Aware of this dynamism and being himself part of this universe, the African participates fully in the achievement of harmony within his physical and spiritual environment. This explains his attitude of reverence towards the elements of nature, an attitude in which Westerners saw as anti-progress and inactive spiritualism. Because, according to Mr. Compagnolo, quoted by Joseph K-Zerbo: "for the African, man should not seek to rise above nature, to dominate it, to subjugate it to his own ends. (…). If the civilization of Europe is called the civilization of man, the African can be called the civilization of nature (…). A completely Africanized humanity would mean the total triumph of nature over man."[26]

Seen in this light, the notion of sustainable development has become, for postmodern societies, a top priority, a pressing necessity that affects all areas of

---

[25] Cheikh Hamidou Kane, in his novel, *L'Aventure Ambigüe*, pp. 83-86, treats Islam as an African religion and contrasts it with Western culture, which he calls very materialistic, with "Islamized" Africa, which he strongly qualifies as spiritualist.
[26] M. Campagnolo cité par Joseph Ki-Zerbo, *Histoire de l'Afrique noire*. Paris: Hatier, 1978, p. 636.

human life. But the motives that lead to it are multiple and vary according to the field in which one is positioned. For some, only the contribution of the so-called exact or experimental sciences counts, in order to achieve the aim. Priority should be given in this case to exact sciences and to the contribution of real experts.[27] For others, all contributions, wherever they come from, are of equal importance, provided they lead us to meet the challenge of realizing the goals of sustainable development.

Thus, if development means: "promise and project of humanism, promotion of the dignity of man linked to the very creative intention of God,"[28] the need and the necessity to engage in concrete actions of Christian witness, in the African context today, are confirmed. This is because, in the context of alienation and oppression of all kinds, nothing seems more urgent than the fact of being recognized as a human being created in the image of God, according to the book of Genesis in chapters 1 and 2.

In order to give back to humanity its true dimension which thereby places it, at the centre of any process of sustainable development, it is the task of Christians, committed to the search for practical solutions, to meet the challenges of an ecological crisis, in close relation with deviant theologies linked to the very controversial and polysemous notions of 'wealth' and 'prosperity', in the African context today.

Some Questions for Reflection

The following three questions show that the problem concerning ecological crisis is an open problem, which cannot be resolved once and for all:

1. What are the elements of your convictions that you want to share with others, with a view to a convictional dialogue aimed at the restoration of divine creation?
2. What are the elements that you consider unique to your convictions and which are capable of restoring constructive relations and our common responsibility, vis-à-vis the ecological crisis which threaten our existence?
3. How can you help your faith community to change destructive attitudes and practices towards the ecological crisis and the theological challenge of understanding the concepts of 'wealth' and 'prosperity'?

---

[27] This is a position largely justified by government policies regarding the granting of graduate scholarships and the disregard that these same colonial governments reserved for studies of social sciences such as philosophy, history, and sociology.
[28] E. J. Penoukou, *Eglises d'Afrique: Propositions pour l'avenir. Paris:* Karthala, 1984, p. 83.

Theological Views and Intentions of Wealth and Prosperity in Modern Africa
Sekenwa Moses Briska

The theological perception of wealth in the scripture can be traced by back to the creation of humankind. God created Adam and Eve and placed them in the Garden of Eden, and said to them, have dominion, take care and eat from the garden and all that is in it (Genesis 1:26-31; 2:15-16). God made everything available to sustain humankind. He commanded them to multiply and subdue and have dominion over everything created. This is an indication that wealth is to be used wisely for God's creative purpose, therefore, it is an aspect of general prosperity of life, and not only in terms of amassing material possessions. God gave them everything including plants, seeds, fruits, beasts, birds, insects; in fact, living and non-living, for humankind to benefit from it (Genesis 1:29-30). Adam was also asked to name all the creatures because he was going to use them for his benefit and to the glory of God, therefore, Adam knew creatures by name for their relationship (Genesis 2:18-20a).

The prosperity gospel preaching can be traced back to the emergence of Pentecostal and Charismatic movements that have taken over the world of Christianity, especially in Africa as a major influence.[1] For precision sake, however, Ferguson's point in this respect is worthwhile: "Pentecostal theology has its roots in various aspects of 19th century fundamentalism in America: Holiness groups which taught that one could receive after conversion an experience of entire sanctification, sometimes called the baptism of the spirit, and an endowment of power by some key leaders such as Charles Finney, Asa Mahan and Phoebe W. Palmer."[2] The church from inception has been operating on the basis of this biblical prophetic history.

Generally, for the mainline, Evangelical and Pentecostal churches, prosperity refers to a person's material possessions as well as general welfare including good health, business success, and academic success. Ojo cites Pastor David Oyedepo of the popular Living Faith Church (a.k.a. Winners Chapel) who understands prosperity as: "a state of well-being in your spirit and body. It is the ability to use God's power to meet every need of men, where, he can enjoy a life of plenty and fulfillment. Prosperity is a state of being successful; it

---

[1] Allan. H. Anderson, 'The newer Pentecostal and Charismatic Churches: The shape of Future Christianity in Africa?' *Pneuma,* 24, No. 2, Fall, 2002, pp. 167-8.
[2] Sinclair B. Ferguson et al. (eds.), *New Dictionary of Theology.* Leicester: Inter-Varsity Press, 1989.

is a life on a big scale".³ Africa, in her poverty-stricken environment, has become susceptible to a different understanding and views of wealth and prosperity gospel messages. This raises the need for the proper development of leaders who will in turn empower members with sound theology that meets the challenges of misleading theologies that do not liberate Africans from their suffering, poverty, underdevelopment, conflicts and spiritual bankruptcy. This can be meaningful if the fight against suffering and poverty alleviation is genuinely pursued with the desire for the fair distribution of wealth within the African continent. In Africa, entrepreneurship is supposed to be for a sustainable society and wealth creation, and should deliberately be integrated into Seminary curricula in order to achieve this goal of empowerment. The message of prosperity is an effort to minimize the gap between the "extremely rich" and "extremely poor" giving the impression that everyone can accumulate wealth and can prosper in life like any other person by being righteous with God is misleading in itself.

Sound theology and the hermeneutics of wealth and prosperity have been hijacked by false interpretations and purposes for selfish material possessions only, instead of focusing on it for human development. Every human being can have access to an improved and quality life by which the most basic human needs such as food, shelter, security, health care, spiritual life, education, clothing and clean environment are adequately met. Pentecostal views and intentions of prosperity and wealth tend to be seen as living an affluent life with material possessions, at the same time experiencing of God's favour, as evidence of one's faith.⁴ The mainline churches' views of wealth and prosperity come with the purpose to serve God and humanity, which is why God created wealth.

Objectives of the Study

The main objective of the study is to ascertain the effect of theological views and intentions of wealth and prosperity in modern Africa. The specific objectives are:
1. To examine the impact of theological views and intentions of wealth accumulation in modern Africa;
2. To determine the level of prosperity preaching in spiritual formation of Christians in Africa;
3. To examine the misleading theologies responsible for suffering and underdevelopment in modern Africa today;

---

[3] M.A. Ojo. In D*iscovering the Other Side: Challenges of Other Religions*, eds. Emiola Nihinlola and Mojisola Olaniyan. Ibadan: Flourish Books, 2004, p. 129.
[4] Allan H. Anderson, "Pentecostalism." In *Global Dictionary of Theology*, ed., William A. Dyrness et al. Nottingham: Inter-Varsity Press, 2008, p. 645.

4. To examine the theological views responsible for the poverty of majority Christians in modern Africa today.

Research Questions
The following are the research questions:
1. What is the impact of theological views and intentions of wealth accumulation in modern Africa?
2. What is the level of prosperity preaching in the spiritual formation of Christians in modern Africa?
3. Do misleading theologies lead to suffering and underdevelopment in modern Africa today?
4. Who is responsible for the poverty of the majority of Christians in modern Africa today?

Conceptual Framework
Theology: Douglas John Hall, defines theology as: "Theology is that ongoing activity of the whole church that aims at clarifying what "gospel" must mean here and now…(it) is thinking about everything all the time."[5] Furthermore, Charles M. Wood also defines theology as "thinking about Christian faith and life and practice, certain ways of forming judgments, certain habits of reflections."[6] Therefore, it is evident that theology can address diverse human conditions, but sound theology must be in accordance with the Word of God and the purpose for which the gospel is given to the world, and not for personal or selfish interests.

Intentions: refers to what people intend to do with what they are doing to get what is being pursued. *Views:* can be defined as the way people see, perceive and understand things their own way. *Wealth:* refers to what a person acquires or has as abundance, resources and material possessions in any form.

Prosperity: refers to a position of a person in terms of success by having property and material possessions.

Theology of Wealth and Prosperity
The impact of theological views and intentions that is focused on wealth accumulation permeates the church in modern Africa. The theological views of mainline and Evangelical/Pentecostal churches on wealth and prosperity are drawn from the scriptures. But emphasis by the Pentecostals is more on the

---

[5] Douglas John Hall, 'What is Theology?' 25, no. 2, p. 177.
[6] Charles M., Wood, *An Invitation to Theological Study.* Valley Forge, PA: Trinity Press International, 1994.

theology of glory instead of the theology of the cross by mainline churches.[7] God in his mercy, not based on any human condition, created physical materials before he created human beings for their sustenance and development in every way (Genesis. 1:26-31). In addition, the scripture also describes Abraham as wealthy with livestock, silver, and gold (Genesis. 13:2). The scripture provides guidance on the purpose and use of wealth: "Honour the Lord with your substance and with the first fruit of all your produce" (Prov. 3:9). Honouring God means glorifying and loving God and caring for the needy and the entire creation. In doing so, "then your barns will be filled with plenty and your vats (containers) will be bursting with wine" (Proverbs. 3:10). Individuals became rich in their hard work, "Isaac sowed seed in that land, and in the same year reaped a hundred-fold. The Lord blessed him" (Genesis 26:12), but the usage must be for larger creation. Furthermore, the scripture states: "But remember the Lord your God, for it is he who gives you power to get wealth, so that he may confirm his covenant that he sower to your ancestors, as he is doing today" (Deuteronomy 8:18). These theological views take into consideration of the entire humankind not only a few individuals. What is the covenant made by God? It is His grace to save humanity for freedom, eternal salvation, care and protection with justice and equality of all people. Therefore, wealth is a blessing for the benefit of all and not a curse.

Views and Intentions of Wealth and Prosperity

Determining the level of prosperity preaching in relation to the spiritual formation of Christians in Africa becomes necessary. It is undoubtedly true that most prosperity gospel preachers tend to play on intelligence with crafty words in manipulating, luring and scaring followers' spiritual and psychological being into uncritical submission considered as obedience to God. The preachers believe in their misleading theologies and messages through their disposition, status and articulation of choice language and words to achieve their intentions of selfish and personal wealth. This leads us to inquire further by saying even though Africa is experiencing and feeling the gravity of global Christianity, which means there are more Christians, it is the poorest continent. The question remains, what kind of Christians or Christianity does Africa have? To answer this question, I borrow from a recent statement by the Bishop of the Roman Catholic Diocese of Oyo, Emmanuel Badejo: "A large part of Christians today are Christians in name, who pursue power, position, privileges. That's not Christianity. And that's where I come to the issue of the prosperity gospel. The prosperity gospel provides cheap solutions to complex realities of life and so many people have heard it. They believe that it is actually possible to have cancer and pray it away when doctors are actually available; that it is possible

---

[7] Allan H. Anderson, 'The newer Pentecostal and Charismatic Churches: The shape of Future Christianity in Africa?' *Pneuma*, 24, No. 2, Fall, 2002, pp. 167-184.

to fail exams, and still become the director of a bank, if you pray enough."[8] Whether a Pentecostal or mainline church, it is evident that any wealth accumulation that is institutionalized, whether by any social class or any category, suggests segregation through an indulgent or permissive demanding of supremacy, instead of the liberating power of God to all humankind.[9] Whenever pastors from all denominations discuss, it is mostly not about how many converts and the renewal of spiritual life of people but about what cars, how many houses, suits, what kind of business and all that makes human life luxurious now.

St. Paul states that in whatever you are doing: "Try and find out what is pleasing to the Lord" (Ephesians. 5:10). This refers to a deep search of the heart and mind regarding relationships, and treating the others respectively, and in the meaning of life. The purpose of wealth and prosperity, according to God's original plan, is for humankind to be sustained, have freedom to be independent-dependent on God's providence, protection, and sustenance. God created human being's first trade or business as farming, which is the tilling of the land in order to have food sufficient to take care of human needs, and for human prosperity, which includes the possessing of properties, health, environment, and relationships with fellow human beings and the natural world creation in general. If Jesus Christ taught Christians to be generous and hospitable to those with whom we live together, our neighbours and even strangers, it means we must have what to give, we must possess something that will enable us to give them. This will include the possession of wealth and properties. Riches is in God's plan for humankind to live a happy life in His grace.

Wealth, Prosperity and Poverty in Modern Africa

It is very important to understand whether misleading theologies are responsible for poverty and underdevelopment in modern Africa today. As stated above, wealth and prosperity refer to having material possessions that make an individual acquire affluence as an indication of comfort and prosperity. Nihinlola asserts that: "The absence of equal distribution of available resources and its concentration in the hands of few individuals is closely connected... and is... responsible for deceit and insincerity on the part of many leaders today in Africa."[10] As Christians we need to keep our treasure in heaven not in this world (Luke 6:19-20). If prosperity is a sign of spirituality,

---

[8] Wilbur O'Donovan, *Biblical Christianity in Modern Africa*. Carlisle: Paternoster Press, 2000.
[9] O. Kalu, 'African Theology, Protestant'. In *Global Dictionary of Theology*, eds. William A. Dyrness and Veil-Matti Kärkkäinen, pp. 10-15.
[10] Emiola Nihinlola, *Integrated Theology and Pastoral Ministry in Africa: International Council for Higher Education*. Bangalore: Theological Trust, 2011, p. 139.

and if spirituality is "any basis, or value, be it of religious, moral, ethical, philosophical or any nature that is concretized as an attitude or spirit or principles from which one's actions flow;"[11] Africa would not be experiencing such extreme poverty, underdevelopment and heinous discrimination between the rich and the poor as it is today.

A popular adage says "wealth is health" and health is a holistic matter that encompasses the spiritual, social, psychological and physical well-being of a person. Poverty, health and hygiene go hand in hand and they affect spiritual and social life of an individual. This means that there is economic poverty as well as spiritual poverty. Nihinlola asserts that: "An economic measure of poverty identifies an income sufficient to provide a minimum level of consumption of goods and services. A sociologic measure of poverty is concerned not with consumption but with social participation. Poverty leads to a person's exclusion from the mainstream way of life and activities in a society"[12] which includes spiritual life. If poverty can have multidimensional implications, so also can wealth have multidimensional implications.

Issues of struggle, hurdles and pains in life which reveal the message of the cross are denied; the intentional lifting up of only the message of glory and not the cross in life can be said to be responsible for poverty in Africa, due to the attitude of not taking responsibility and acting according to God's will by being creative, innovative and productive. There can be a series of questions that prick people's conscience in regards to wealth. First, whether wealth can be considered a sin, curse or blessings. Wealth in itself, is not a sin and cannot be viewed as a curse, otherwise God would not have entrusted its possession when He created it for humankind to care and use it for His glory and for the sustenance of human existence (Genesis 1:26-31; 2:15-16). In our world today, wealth is a source of economy that helps to facilitate the proclamation of the Good News to the world. Nihinlola asserts that poverty of wealth has affected the spread of the gospel in Nigeria: "The growth of some of the churches plateaued and their church planting efforts became weak because of luck of resources to buy and use more evangelistic equipment to organize more campaigns to plant more churches".[13] We are God's children, who have been entrusted the management of the garden. It means that there is a sense of privilege and responsibility in the accumulation of wealth; "Since God owns everything, we will share in everything (1 Corinthians 3:21-23)! Our human mind cannot grasp what this means but we can be sure it will be better than

---

[11] Samuel P. Gwimi, 'The Significance of African Spirituality in the realization of Vision 2063,' *Journal of West African Association of Theological Institutions, Politics and the Church in Africa,* 2017, p. 139.

[12] Emiola Nihinlola, *Integrated Theology and Pastoral Ministry in Africa: International Council for Higher Education.* Bangalore: Published by Theological Trust, 2011, p. 134.

[13] Emiola Nihinlola, *Theology Under the Mango Tree: A Handbook of African Theology.* Lagos: Print & Manufacturing, 2013, p. 135.

anything we have ever imagined (1Corinthians 2:9; Revelation 21:6-7)."[14] Our responsibility lies in the fact that whenever Jesus enters a person's life, everything changes, our selfish greedy life will change into generosity: "Zachaeus stood there and said to Lord, "Look, half of my possession, Lord, I will give to the poor, and if I have defrauded anyone of anything, I will pay back four times as much (Luke 19:8). Therefore, we can use our wealth to effect and empower the lives of others for the good.

The poverty of resources leads to a poverty of leadership that also results into other kinds of poverty, such as that of dignity, minds, progress, health, physical, environment and spirituality.[15] The Bible speaks of stewardship of wealth and human life as well as an indication that wealth is not evil, but rather a gift from God to be used for His glory and human development. Wealth is meant to improve human lives and for the transformation of humanity and creation in general. Nihinlola used a popular statement on mission of the church that says: "Money is the vehicle of mission", such as "church planting and growth using expensive evangelistic methods of technology."[16] Today, challenged as we are by the global capitalistic life of materialism and consumerism competitions, how would the church survive and continue to proclaim its missions? It is acceptable to be good, rich, and happy and live a peaceful life but the prosperity gospel uses Jesus as magical, a cut-and-paste miraculous quick rich agent, therefore, making salvation a commodity to be bought and sold cheaply without any hope earned through sacrifice.

Modern Africa and the Effect of Wealth and Prosperity

Africans are not lazy but as subsistent farmers they struggle to grow their economy and lifestyle. Modernity in some way has brought a negative impact on the lifestyle of hard work whereby someone can sit, control and acquire wealth by just talking and manipulating a system. Re-invigorating African productive life must come into play in its real sense of communal care and the empowerment of nature. Traditionally, Africans trained their people, both female and male, from childhood through initiation rites, to develop them to be physically strong, intellectually and mentally sound, to enable them to protect their land, take care of themselves and their families, and be self-sufficient in every way. This training includes spiritual formation which liberates people to live as free people in their context. As a result, one would expect today that African Christians can draw from this positive culture in their proclamation of the gospel of salvation. A gospel message is meant to liberate human society

---

[14] Wilbur O'Donovan, *Biblical Christianity in African Perspective*. Carlisle: Paternoster Press, 1996, p. 112.
[15] Emiola Nihinlola, *Theology Under the Mango Tree: A Handbook of African Theology*. Lagos: Print & Manufacturing, 2013, p. 136.
[16] Nihinlola, p. 140.

into spiritual, economic and political freedom in accordance with the Word of God (Luke 4:16-19).[17] Today, the concept of a prosperity gospel has become a private enterprise instead of a community affair. People have been turned into a commodity prepared to be used in exchange of the Word of God with money or material possessions and other evil vices.[18] Africa must get away from this mentality of dependency that counters productive life because such a cheap way of living does not represent God's creative purpose for human beings. The culture of a communal sense of spiritual, economic, social and general prosperity is intertwined, and can make Africa live out a true Christian life.[19]

There is conflict in the cultures of individual and communal interests. Today, in this Symposium we are concerned with the prosperity gospel preaching which is more or less materially focused due to several factors:

- One, we can see few individuals that are getting richer at the expense of the majority of poor people;
- Two, Christian spiritual formation seems to be based on falsehood and is unbiblical therefore, misleading the majority by the so-called few chosen ones as leaders;
- Three, there seems to be no sense of communal care and empowering culture according to the African culture of training the younger ones for self-supporting, family caring, for the courage to face the challenges of the world, and the protection of the family and society;
- Four, the concern for the safety of the generality of creation has been neglected and the world is being destroyed amidst the so-called religious people who are after God's heart but have no concern about God's creation.

The indigenous leadership of the mainline churches' preaching focuses only on heaven and has not shown enough ministry that encompasses salvation, freedom and empowering culture for self-sustaining, self-propagating and self-governance that reveals a life of abundance (John 10:10). Africa as a community-oriented society is struggling with a false identity, and the emerging external forces of globalization and modernity that focus on the ideology of individualism.

The purpose of God's provision of wealth in Africa is destroyed by misinterpretation in the prosperity gospel, using misleading theologies that focus on an endless accumulation and not giving away. This is a sign of

---

[17] Chinonyerem Chijioke Ekebuisi, 'Colonial Power, Garrick Braide and the Campaign Against Liquor Trade that Devalues Moral, Ethical and Spiritual Foundation for Prosperous Nigeria', ed. *Journal of West African Association of Theological Institutions, Politics and the Church in Africa,* 2017, pp. 94-95.

[18] Ekebuisi, 94.

[19] J. Kwabena Asamoah-Gyadu, "Essential Features of Misleading theologies in Africa." In Bosela E. Eale and Njoroge J. Ngige (eds.) *Addressing Contextual Misleading Theologies in Africa Today.* Oxford: Regnum Books International, 2020, pp. 12-43.

selfishness, greed and a discriminatory concept of materialism as a sign of faith. This disregards the responsibility of the Christian and instead, members are always required to sow seeds and reap abundant blessings without any call to care and support the needy. Mega-conferences are mostly organized with the intention of collecting more offerings of financial gain in order to get wealthy. This prosperity gospel is influenced by too many factors within and outside the African continent.[20] Africa is considered today as dark, poor, poverty-stricken and undeveloped. The measure of a wealthy society should not be on the accumulation of property, but by how people are living, whether peacefully, healthily, joyfully and happily in all spheres of life.

It is evident that some churches in Nigeria are following a secular understanding of wealth, whereby, it is used to enrich the church elites, clerics or church leaders over against their poor followers. Africa's underdevelopment due to a search for power and control by all means results in greed, selfishness, and individualism. This idea moves away from family care and participatory relationship. This attitude "explains the various conflicts across the African Continent in particular and the world at large."[21] As a result, the majority of people in modern Africa are living in abject poverty.

Research Design

A survey research design was adopted for this study. A descriptive survey research design is the systematic collection of data in a standardized form from an identifiable population or representative.[22] This design was adopted for this study because it intensively described and analysed the role of theological views and intentions of wealth and prosperity in modern Africa. According to Cohen, Manion, and Morrison, for any meaningful and representative research, a sample of at least above 10% is representative enough of a larger population.[23] Sampling methods involved taking at random a predetermined quantity from a batch of the same kind, a quantity considered adequate and representative of the whole population. The targeted populations in this research study were 150 pastors who were divided into the two theological views of the mainline and Evangelical/Pentecostal churches as the independent variables, while views in relation to wealth and prosperity in modern Africa

---

[20] A. O. Balcomb, "African Theology, Evangelical, Contextual." In *Global Dictionary of Theology*, ed. William A. Dyrness and Veil-Matti Kärkkäinen, pp. 7-10.
[21] Samuel P. Gwimi, 'The Significance of African Spirituality in the realization of Vision 2063.' *Journal of West African Association of Theological Institutions, Politics and the Church in Africa*, 2017, p. 49.
[22] L. R. Gay, Geoffrey, E. Mills. and Peter W. Airasien, *Educational research: competencies for Analysis and Applications*. 10th ed. Hoboken, NJ: Pearson Education, 2012, p. 183.
[23] L. Manion, L. Cohen and K. Morrison, *Research methods in education*. 6th ed. New York: Routledge, 2013.

were the dependent variables. Out of 150 questionnaires distributed which constituted 100%, 124 were returned representing 75%.

Instrument of Data Collection

The respondents were asked on a five-point Likert scale where 5 is strongly agree, 4 agree, 3 neutral, 2 disagree and 1 strongly disagree, to state how they score with the given statements on theological views and intentions of wealth and prosperity in modern Africa. The questionnaires whose content comprises of closed-ended questions were used to collect data. Questionnaires were administered to pastors, Bishops, prophets, Reverends, apostles and evangelists within the two main divided views regarding theological views and intentions of wealth and prosperity in modern Africa.

Data Presentation and Analysis

Table 1: The mean and standard deviations of the respondents on theological views and intentions of wealth accumulation in modern Africa:

Decision	N	Total	Mean	SD
1. Wealth and prosperity are righteous signs of blessings (Accept)	124	450	3.63	0.45
2. There are genuine theologies that lift up decent wealth and prosperity among Christians in Africa (Accept)	124	434	3.50	0.50
3. The wealthier you are the more Christian you are (Accept)	124	455	3.67	0.47
4. Sound theologies can change Africa's condition for the better (Accept)	124	422	3.40	0.49
		G. Mean	**3.55**	

The data in table 1 shows that the respondents accepted items 1, 2, 3, and 4 with respective mean score of 3.63, 3.50, 3.67 and 3.40 and standard deviation scores of 0.45, 0.50, 0.47 and 0.49. The items were accepted because the mean scores were up to and above 2.50 mean cut-off mark. It implies that there is a relationship between theological views and intentions of wealth accumulation in modern Africa.

Table 2: The mean and standard deviations of the respondents on prosperity preaching in the spiritual formation of Christians in Africa:

Decision	N	Total	Mean	SD
5. Prosperity gospel is biblical and liberating (Accept)	124	471	3.80	0.40
6. Prosperity gospel empowers people economically, socially and politically (Accept)	124	476	3.84	0.03

Decision	N	Total	Mean	SD
7. Prosperity gospel enables genuine spiritual formation (Accept)	124	383	3.09	0.26
8. All people who listen to the prosperity gospel prosper (Accept)	124	496	4.00	0.00
		G. Mean	**3.68**	

The data in table 2 shows that the respondents accepted items 5, 6, 7 and 8 with respective mean score of 3.80, 3.84, 3.09 and 4.00 and standard deviation scores of 0.40, 0.03, 0.26 and 0.00. The items were accepted because the mean scores were up to and above 2.50 mean cut-off mark. It implies that there is a relationship between prosperity preaching in the spiritual formation of Christians in Africa.

Decision	N	Total	Mean	SD
5. Prosperity gospel is biblical and liberating (Accept)	124	471	3.80	0.40
6. Prosperity gospel empowers people economically, socially and politically (Accept)	124	476	3.84	0.03
7. Prosperity gospel enables genuine spiritual formation (Accept)	124	383	3.09	0.26
8. All people who listen to the prosperity gospel prosper (Accept)	124	496	4.00	0.00
		G. Mean	**3.68**	

Table 3: The mean and standard deviations of the respondents on whether misleading theologies lead to suffering and underdevelopment in modern Africa today:

Decision	N	Total	Mean	SD
9. Wealth and prosperity are righteous signs of blessings (Accept)	124	476	3.84	0.03
10. There are genuine theologies that lift up decent wealth and prosperity among Christians in Africa (Accept)	124	470	3.79	0.04
11. The wealthier you are the more Christian you are (Accept)	124	489	3.94	0.02
12. Sound theologies can change Africa's condition (Accept)	124	483	3.90	0.03
		G. Mean	**3.87**	

The data in table 3 shows that the respondents accepted items 9, 10, 11 and 12 with respective mean score of 3.84, 3.79, 3.94 and 3.90 and standard deviation scores of 0.03, 0.04, 0.02 and 0.03. The items were accepted because the mean scores were up to and above 2.50 mean cut-off mark. It implies that wealth and prosperity are righteous signs of blessings to the majority, there are genuine theologies can lift up decent wealth and prosperity among Christians in

Africa; while to others the wealthier you are the more Christian you are and sound theologies can change Africa's condition for better by organizing seminars and workshops regarding theological issues on wealth and prosperity.

Table 4: The mean and standard deviations of the respondents on who is responsible for the poverty of majority of Christians in modern Africa today:

Decision	N	Total	Mean	SD
13. African clergies are richer than their church members (Accept)	124	406	3.27	0.04
14. African clergies preach prosperity instead of Jesus (Accept)	124	496	4.00	0.00
15. Modern African Christians yearn for prosperity gospel than the true gospel of liberation and freedom through Jesus (Accept)	124	489	3.94	0.02
16. The church in Africa is planning to eradicate poverty (Accept)	124	422	3.40	0.49
		G. Mean	**3.87**	

The data in table 4 shows that the respondents accepted items 13, 14, 15 and 16 with respective mean score of 3.27, 4.00, 3.94 and 3.40 and standard deviation scores of 0.04, 0.00, 0.02 and 0.49. The items were accepted because the mean scores were up to and above 2.50 mean cut-off mark. This indicated that clergies are richer that their church members because of their negative intentions on wealth accumulation ad prosperity, Christians in Africa yearn for the prosperity gospel rather than the true gospel of liberation and freedom through Jesus. The church in Africa is planning to eradicate poverty since such programmes are aimed at adding to the value of knowledge regarding the best theological views concerning wealth and prosperity in modern Africa and the revival we thirst for.

Discussion on Study Findings

The question for objective 1 was designed to understand the impact of theological views and intentions of wealth accumulation in modern Africa. With descriptive statistics, the mean responses for variables from research questions 1 was above 2.5 at 5 point Likert scale which confirm that respondents agreed to issues raised in the questionnaire.

The question for objective 2 was designed to determine the level of prosperity preaching in spiritual formation of Christians in Africa. With descriptive statistics, the mean responses for variables from research questions 2 was above 2.5 at 5 point Likert scale, which confirm that respondents agreed to issues raised in the questionnaire.

The question for objective 3 was designed to examine the misleading theologies responsible for suffering and underdevelopment in modern Africa today. With descriptive statistics, the mean responses for variables from research questions 3 was above 2.5 at 5 point Likert scale, which confirm that respondents agreed to issues raised in the questionnaire.

The question for objective 4 was designed to examine the theological views responsible for the poverty of Christians in modern Africa today. With descriptive statistics, the mean responses for variables from research questions 4 was above 2.5 at 5 point Likert scale, which confirms that respondents agreed to issues raised in the questionnaire.

Summary

The result of question one reveals in the church there is a relationship between theological views and intentions on wealth accumulation in modern Africa. The result of question two reveals in the church that prosperity preaching influences spiritual formation of Christians in Africa. The result of question three reveals that misleading theologies are responsible for the suffering and underdevelopment in modern Africa today. The result of question four reveals in the church that theological views are responsible for the poverty of the majority Christians in modern Africa today.

Recommendations

1. Africans must not deny the fact that God can act in ways that we in mainline churches cannot understand fully.
2. Africans do not have all the answers, but they need to be open to surprises and not lose focus.
3. Africans must engage in teaching and empowering our members with sound theologies that are biblically rooted to liberate and capture the hearts of the younger generations.
4. Africans need to be spiritual both theoretical and practical, and we must intentionally speak against these vices all the more.
5. Programmes like this aim at adding to the value of knowledge regarding sound theological views concerning wealth and prosperity in modern Africa and the genuine revival African people thirst for.
6. Africans should be critical of situations by their freedom to ask questions with wisdom, in order to access better solutions to their problems and needs.
7. Africans need to dismantle and eradicate the concept of blind obedience in order to understand their conditions and seek direction from God through Jesus Christ under the guidance of the Holy Spirit for proper discernment.

Conclusion

Based on the literature review and above empirical discussion, misleading theologies have taken root not only among Pentecostals as it is always assumed, but also in the evangelical and mainline churches consciously or unconsciously. Question three surprised me because it was supposed to be rejected, but it was accepted. This proves that misleading theologies on prosperity gospel have permeated even the mainline and Orthodox churches.

The Bible teaches us to seek first the Kingdom of God, and all other things will be given to us (Matthew. 6:33), which means riches are not a sin but should be used for the glory of God and not to the detriment of other people. Today, it is the contrary that we proclaim. We start with the issues of wealth before blessings come, or we do it with the intention of getting wealthy and prosperous, and do not seek the Kingdom of God as the first thing to do. This shows our disobedience to God, because a misconception of wealth separates people from God.

Biblical texts such as Mark 10:29-30; 3 John verse 2, stress the reality of Jesus stating that whoever leaves everything and follows him, will receive hundredfold now. Jesus teaches us to pray that, "God gives us daily bread (Matthew. 5:11). Jesus says we "will not get back very much more in this age, and in the age to come eternal life" (Luke 18: 30). Jesus also says in the gospel of John, whatever we ask for in his name we shall get and our joy will be complete (John 16:23-24). Living godly in Christ will be persecuted (2 Timothy 3:12; 1 Thessalonians 3:3; Romans 5:3). "For the Lord disciplines those whom he loves, and chastises every child whom he accepts" (Hebrews. 12:6). Job says; *shall we receive the good at the hand of God, and not receive the bad*? (Job 2:10). In all of these, where is the focus of the Word of God?

PART THREE

Ecclesiological Responses to Wealth and Prosperity in Africa

Ecclesiological Responses to Preaching of Prosperity
Christopher Aigbadumah

The African church had not lacked in contentious issues such as happened in the past with its identity crisis, and claims of it being a foreign religion. Over time, this claim was countered by a strong Christian presence on the continent, validated by the founding and growth of numerous African indigenous churches and the presence of homegrown theologians who promoted African Christian thought.

In recent years, however, the Church in Africa has faced threats of deviant or misleading theologies, ranging from syncretism in some indigenous churches, to counterfeit teachings imported from outside the continent. Of particular interest is the health and wealth gospel, sometimes referred to as the prosperity gospel.

The kernel of this teaching is that God wills all of his children to live healthy and wealthy lives with boundless happiness, clearly as evidence of their faith. This teaching has been widely accepted largely by the Pentecostal churches in Africa, where clergy and laymen have adopted a lifestyle of opulence in the midst of abject poverty ravaging the African continent.

The wide acceptance of the prosperity gospel amongst some African churches may be attributed to the grinding poverty and deprivations juxtaposed with the affluence of a very few in the society. Added to this is the culture that gives prominence to the wealthy and influential in the society, irrespective of the sources of their wealth. The influence of present day "*African politics*", the disposition of the ruling class that has encouraged corruption and ostentatious living among the elites, also contribute to the insatiable quest for wealth. The clergy in some of these contexts has bought in a doctrine of greed over creed, and promoted the health and wealth gospel.

This study is an attempt to examine the challenge the prosperity gospel poses to the African churches at large, and how the church can respond and address some of these challenges. The rapid growth of Christianity in Third World countries and its decline in Europe and America is a widely acknowledged fact. Andrew Walls remarked that "the centre of gravity in the Christian world has shifted inexorably Southward, to Africa and Latin America."[1] This is in conformity with the renowned Kenyan scholar, John Mbiti, who observed "the centres of the church's universality (are) no longer in

---

[1] Phillip Jenkins, *The Next Christendom: The Coming of Global Christianity.* New York: Oxford University Press, 2007, p. 1.

Geneva, Rome, Athens, Paris, London, New York, but Kinshasa, Buenos Aires, Addis Ababa and Manila."[2]

It is remarkable also that this growth happened in the decades of a century characterized by ravaging wars and conflicts, famine, poor economic planning, monoculture economies that suffer often from the vagaries of demand and price manipulations, and natural disasters. Other factors such as inept and corrupt leadership, political upheavals, the poor utilization of resources, nepotism and bad governance that exploit and impoverish the populace (sometimes creating two distinct classes of the extremely rich and extremely poor in the same society), are responsible for the underdevelopment of the African nations. In spite of these negative trends, Christianity experienced a boom, surviving and expanding astronomically.

It is also a widely acknowledged fact that much of this growth accounted for in these contexts happen in the newer churches of Pentecostal, Charismatic and indigenous strands. These churches are reputed for their spirituality, vibrancy, unstructured liturgical practices and are champions of contextualized Christianity. These churches address issues in their particular contexts, as against what obtained in the mission churches of yore that stood aloof from contextual, cultural or existential issues that affected adherents or converts to the faith. Indigenous Christians here have appropriated the Christian faith as their own just as it was with their traditional religions, and no longer see it as the 'White man's religion.' They have domesticated the gospel of Jesus Christ in the African context. However, as it happens in nature, growth as observed in these churches is not without its challenges. One of these has to do with the content of Christianity practised in these contexts. Some of these churches have inadvertently slipped into syncretism, i.e. the acceptance and practice of unwholesome and unorthodox doctrines. They have left their physical doors open for new members which account for their numerical growth and large membership. They have also left their 'spiritual' doors open inadvertently, and are receptive to all manner of doctrines and practices that are not in tandem with orthodox Christian faith or 'faith once delivered unto the saints' (Jude 1:3). These churches have drifted from the truth and are 'carried about with every wind of doctrine' (Ephesians 4:14).

The Bible Verses Used for Deviation Variant Messages

> I can't believe your fickleness –how easily you have turned traitor to him who called you by the grace of Christ, by embracing a variant message! It is not a minor variation, you know; it is completely other, an alien message, a no message, a lie about God. (Galatians 1:7).

---

[2] Ibid., p. 2.

It is the matter of variance or deviation from the centrality of the gospel of Jesus that is the focus of this paper. The degree of variance is dependent on the extent of departure or deviation from the truth or orthodoxy. As one writer stated, 'These deceivers go out into the world with a teaching that is not of Christ. This teaching is perilous in that it separates men from God. Jesus came to tell us the truth about God, man, sin, and salvation, but these teachers come to tell lies about God, man, sin, and salvation-and so their ministry of deception is completely antithetical to Jesus ministry of truth.'[3] The drift from God-centred theology to other worldly-centred theology and philosophy is of a grave concern to contemporary Christianity.

Clarification of Concepts

Ecclesiology – "In Christian theology, ecclesiology is the study of the Christian church, the origins of Christianity, its relationship to Jesus; its role in salvation, its polity, its discipline, its eschatology, and its leadership."[4] Wayne Grudem defines the church "as the community of all true believers for all time."[5] By this he refers to "to all whom Christ died to redeem, all those who are saved by the death of Christ." In other words, the church refers to the 'congregation' or 'assembly' of all of God's people. It may also refer to a community of believers domiciled in space and time, such as in a region or nation. The concept of an African Church as used in this context may therefore apply to the conglomeration of churches in Africa, irrespective of their beliefs, sect or denomination.

Prosperity Gospel – *Christianity Today*, a popular Christian magazine in America from where the prosperity gospel originated, labels it as 'an aberrant theology that teaches God rewards faith-and hefty tithing with financial blessings.'[6] Invariably, anyone who is poor is considered to be either lacking in faith or under a curse. In this regard, it's 'the doctrine that God wants people to prosper, especially financially. Adherents of the prosperity gospel believe that wealth is a sign of God's blessing and the poor are poor because of the lack of faith.'[7] The prosperity gospel is centred on the comfort and ease of Christians rather than projecting the person and works of Jesus Christ. The quest for abundant life, which is the thrust of the prosperity gospel, is often misinterpreted and carried to the extreme in these contexts, such that it now

---

[3] http://www.9marks.org/article/what-does-2-john-have-to-teach-us-about-partnering- Accessed 09/10/2020.
[4] https://www.en.m.wikipedia.org>wiki>Ecclesiology. Accessed 07/10/2020
[5] Wayne Grudem, *Systematic Theology: An Introduction to Biblical Doctrine.* Nottingham: Inter-Varsity Press, 1994, p. 853.
[6] https://www.christianitytoday.com/ct/topics/p/prosperity-gospel/ Accessed 9/10/2020
[7] James N. Amanze, "How Prosperous is the Prosperity Gospel? An examination of the Impacts of the Theology of Prosperity in Africa from a Sociological Perspective." In Samson Adetunji Fatokun et al., eds. *African Christianity in Local and Global Contexts.*

amounts to an abuse or profanation of the authentic gospel. It promotes an unbridled craving for material wealth at the expense of the thorough spiritual formation of the adherents. Their primary desire is not to possess the mind of Christ in all things, but the riches and success of the world.

Seed Faith – other components of the prosperity gospel includes the seed faith propagation. Its emphasis is that we can materialize our hopes of dreams of success, prosperity, and abundance by sowing our best financial seed. Passages such as 2 Corinthians 9:6-15, and Galatians 6:7-9 are often cited, though seriously out of context. We are told that we have the potential within us, and if we will release it, God will make it grow. All too often, we are told that giving beyond our means to a faith preacher, pastor or church leader activates such faith.[8]

Dominion Theology – The prosperity preachers emphasize that the prosperity gospel is congruent with the original plan of God for man prior to the fall at the Garden of Eden to live a rich life of abundance, wherein he exercised dominion over the entire created realm. The dominion theology is rooted in their interpretation of Genesis 1:28, 'And God blessed them, and God said unto them, Be fruitful, and multiply and replenish the earth, and subdue, and have dominion over the fish of the sea, and over the fowl of the air, and over every living thing that move upon the earth.' Dominion is interpreted from the perspective of acquisition of material possessions, where the individual becomes prosperous because he has exercised dominion over the natural and spiritual elements and has become rich materially. Dominion is thus defined from the material perspective, as the Christian's ability to subjugate the forces of lack and poverty in order to become rich in his context. Oftentimes, testimonies are given in these churches of how much is gained at little or no effort, all in the spirit of exercising the dominion principle.

Prosperity Gospel as an Aberration – The prosperity theology as earlier noted, is steeped in crass materialism and rooted in the gratification of material existence. Gary Marxey said of the contemporary Nigerian church, particularly of the Pentecostal strand, that the focus has shifted from "unmistakable God-centredness to a disturbing self-centredness. The focus has shifted from surrender to God, to the cajoling or manipulating of God for the fulfillment of personal desires. Faith as simple trust in a Heavenly Father has turned into inappropriate demandingness, where faith is seen as a tool for obtaining material gain. The primary aim is no longer spiritual transformation for a holy heaven, but rather strategic positioning for earthly comfort. In short, the Nigerian Church has become worldly-minded and earthly centred."[9] African Christianity is notable for addressing contextual issues of existential concerns. However, it is as though Christianity here exists only for problem-solving or

---

[8] Gary S. Maxey and Peter Ozodo, *The Seduction of the Nigerian Church.* Lagos: WATS Publications, 2017, p.101
[9] Ibid., p. 84.

providing a magic wand to becoming rich and happy. It is neither to transform to Christ-likeness as followers of Christ that adherents of the faith seek here, nor to become true disciples, but on how to become wealthy and successful. The African Church should rise to defend the claims of the authentic gospel, push back and address cases of misleading theologies that are rampant in the African context.

Origin and Introduction of Prosperity Gospel in the African Context

The prosperity gospel has its roots in the camp meetings and healing revivals in the early and mid-20th century America. This brand of contemporary gospel was popularized by popular preachers like E.W Kenyon, Kenneth Hagin, Norman Vincent Peale, Kenneth Copeland, Fred Price and other prominent American televangelists. The prosperity gospel crept into African Christianity sometime in the late 1970s, as international travels afforded African Christian ministers the opportunity to interact with American ministers and churches, particularly of the Faith Movement strand. As Gbile Akani relates on the influence of the prosperity gospel on contemporary Nigerian Christianity: "It came through free books and tapes imported to us from America. It came as several of our brothers began to copy and indeed preach messages of those preachers from abroad verbatim. Our design of ministries changed into personally owned works. Our method of fund raising changed with superficial and outrageous seed faith theories."[10] The imported prosperity gospel gradually displaced the burgeoning indigenous Christianity that had appropriated and contextualized the Christian faith in a way fitting to her culture, without necessarily compromising the essence of the Christian faith. This brand of gospel came as a third force impacting Christianity in Africa.

Of particular interest is a shift in theological emphasis from an 'other-worldly' outlook in life, to one that emphasizes 'this worldly' or 'here and now': "The gradual emergence of an increasingly self-centered quasi-biblical and quasi-ethical Christianity was clearly evident as we moved into the '80s and '90s."[11] It is the inconsistencies, brazen hypocritical practices, immoral tendencies, and unbridled and insatiable quest to have wealth and other good things of this life, and most often at the expense of the impoverished membership, that is worrisome about the prosperity gospel. It does not depict the simplicity and ethos entrenched in the gospel of Jesus Christ, who told a would-be follower that 'foxes have holes, the birds of the air have nests, but the Son of man does not have where to lay His head' (Matthew 8:20). The teachings in these Pentecostal and Charismatic churches are most times permissive and appealing to the rich, who are not questioned about the sources of their wealth, or made to feel guilty for possessing stupendous wealth in the

---

[10] Ibid., p. 7.
[11] Ibid., p. 59.

midst of stark poverty in their environment. The teachings here make them feel secure and aspire for a more through 'seed faith' and generous giving and contributions to church programmes and projects. They are told they could be enriched the more. These churches boast of the crème de la crème of the society, the rich and powerful, the super civil servants, and the professionals. This access to the rich and power in the society further influences the leadership of these churches, who would want to rub shoulders with, and emulate the lifestyles of the 'big men' among them.

Factors Contributing to Preaching of Prosperity Gospel in Africa

1. Ease of Receiving Gospel Call

One factor that has led to the accelerated growth of the Pentecostal and Charismatic churches, aside from the attractiveness and relief sought from the prosperity gospel, is the ease with which many pastors and founders established new churches under the guise that they have received calls into the ministry. In the past, those who received the call into the ministry had to have confirmation from their churches authenticating their call, were sent to theological institutions for training, and upon completion of their training, were ordained. In some cases, they served under the tutelage of senior ministers in the ministry while learning the ropes. In this way, the integrity, essence and focus of ministry was maintained. Unfortunately, it is not so anymore.

2. Poorly Trained Clergy from Quack Theological Institutions

In addition to the above is a plethora of unaccredited and ill-equipped theological degree-awarding institutions, churning out 'uncircumcised' and half-baked pastors and leaders. 'Very sub-standard theological schools began to emerge, in too many cases, offering "doctorates" in exchange either for money, or for a few days of uncredited resident study. At the heart was the growing focus on self-centredness, where virtually everything revolved around self-advancement and self-governance. In addition, adopting life practices by blindly copying others without seeking to find the biblical bases for actions seduced many from the path of right theology. Lack of proper training of pastors and church leaders led to all kinds of syncretism.'[12]

3. Lack of Ethical Standards

With graduates from these quack institutions, the flood gates are flung open to allow in all manner of preachers and peddlers of the prosperity gospel; people with little or no theological training who had not seen the four walls of a

---

[12] Ibid., p. 60.

seminary. 'Unfortunately, however, in the Nigerian society, and even in Africa generally, pastors, Reverends, apostles, prophets, evangelists, and other ecclesiastical titles have been hijacked by crooks, criminals, reprobates and the like'[13] These men are laws unto themselves and are accountable to no other persons within their setting but themselves. They are highly feared and revered, almost like cultic figures, in their churches. They are not the servant leaders that Jesus Christ recommended for His Church. They are poor interpreters of the Bible, not possessing the requisite hermeneutical skills for their job.

It is apparent that they are in only for the benefits and their selfish ends, inspired by greed, and not the creed of the calling. According to one of Nigeria's Christian expositors, "The charlatans have come; money-changers have set up their tables, so to say, in the sanctuary; cheap grace, that has no responsibilty for personal holiness and victory over sin and self, has been preached and aired over the airwaves."[14]

4. Commercialization of the Gospel

The gospel is now considered as a commercial enterprise in some of these churches, where the principles and practices of commerce are adopted. Huge billboards featuring advertisements of ministers and their wives as brands are erected on popular streets in African cities, selling as it were, their popular brands. As one American artist puts it, "modern Christianity feels like a sales pitch more than anything else. It is like they are selling a product: The really good-looking pastor with his wife and his beautiful kids, and they seem so happy. It is almost like they're selling, 'if you buy these rules and you do what we do, you can also be like this.'"[15]

Some Effects of the Prosperity Gospel on Churches in African Context

One of the major effects of the prosperity gospel on contemporary African Christianity is the drift from the traditions and orthodoxy of the Christian faith. The drift is from Christ-centredness, to a more materialistic type of faith that rewards faithful adherents with material wealth. African Christianity had contended in the past with the challenge of colonialism and neo-colonialism, and in some contexts, the repudiation of Christianity by socialism or communism. The major challenge, however, was syncretism, as some African converts insisted in carrying over into their new found faith some relics of their African culture and religion. In the past four decades, however, the challenge to

---

[13] Samson Kolawole Oyeku, "African Christianity and Ecclesiastical Corruption: Nigeria as a Study Case." In Samson Adetunji Fatokun et al., eds. *African Christianity in Local and Global Contexts,* p. 426.
[14] Gary S. Maxey and Peter Ozodo, *The Seduction of the Nigerian Church,* p. 10.
[15] https://churchleaders.com/news/329451-spencer-chmaberlain-they-used-to-be-a-christian-band-and-then-christians-failed-them.html Accessed 10/11/2020

African Christianity has been American materialism in the form of the prosperity gospel. Unfortunately, it is now noticeable that a significant segment of the Christian church in this country is gradually but steadily departing from the basic goals of Christianity. The entire church is in danger of losing its basic direction. The result is that increasingly, many Christians are living in ways not in keeping with the standards of the scriptures. Materialism is enthroned, and sin is tolerated, while holiness is largely ignored. With a focus being placed on the popularity of the preachers, the biblical life-style is largely forgotten. Indeed it is very painful to see churches in our country today with no marked change in the ways and lives of the people."[16]

The perception that the good things of life can come as a windfall by possessing the right kind of faith has bred a generation of slothful Christians. It is a Christianity of something coming one's way all for little or no effort, but by making the right confession of faith and sowing the necessary seed faith, money. There is no question that it has seriously tainted authentic Christianity, leaving the impression in the popular minds that all church leaders – pastors, priests, Bishops, theologians, lay administrators – are "making money off the Cross," thus accommodating their own interests and greed at the expense of those they purport to serve. This negative perception rubs off on all as Christians. It makes others outside the faith to reason that Christian leaders are all out for the money.

Prosperity Gospel's Resonance with Africa Traditional Religion

The prosperity gospel is now the most popular version of Christianity in the global South. While writing on the harm to the body of Christ by the peddlers of the health and wealth gospel, the Vatican representative of the Roman Catholic Church, expressed concerns about the well-known theological current emerging from the neo-Pentecostal evangelical movements thus, "The risk of this form of religious anthropocentrism, which puts humans and their well-being at the centre, is that it transforms God into a power at our service, the Church into a supermarket of faith, and religion into a utilitarian phenomenon that is eminently sensationalist and pragmatic.[17]

It is believed that one reason that prosperity gospel resonates with Africans is its anthropocentric emphasis, rather than the theocentric focus of true Christianity. This anthropocentric perspective is shared with African Traditional Religion which centres on man. "The whole emphasis is upon man gaining power needed to live a good life. Life centres on man and his interests

---

[16] Gary S. Maxey and Peter Ozodo, *The Seduction of the Nigerian Church*, p. 16.
[17] https://churchleaders.com/news/329453-the-prosperity-gospel-criticized-by-the-vatican.html Accessed 11/11/2020

and needs. It is as if God exists for the sake of man."[18] It further stated that such a theology makes God in the image and likeness of the people and their situation, and not according to the biblical model and causes its adherents to view poverty, sickness and unhappiness as a lack of faith.

Ecclesiological Responses to Complexities of the Prosperity Gospel

There are numerous ways that the aberrant theology of the prosperity gospel can be addressed in the African context. It should be acknowledged, however, that the aberrant nature of this form of theology is not altogether new to the Christian faith. Christian history has been replete with variant or aberrant theologies or heresies over time.

One response to the gospel of excess or prosperity is to speak out and condemn it, as widely and publicly as possible. This is an urgent part of our witness in this money-drenched and money- obsessed culture, particularly with the attacks made in general against the Christian faith, and the tendency of the media to lump all into the same category, both of faith and of practice (or malpractice). The church at large should rise up and denounce those practices that are not in congruence with biblical faith. The Assemblies of God, for example, in an official denominational statement, stated that behind the Word of Faith's attempt to 'use God's ability and power' is a mindset in which man is in charge rather than God. This is an expression of secular humanism "which puts man in the position of using God, rather than man surrendering himself to be used of God."[19] Right Bible believing and teaching churches have the responsibility to both create an awareness of the dangers of seductive teachings in the body of Christ, and to counter these teachings with the right teachings of the authentic gospel of Jesus Christ. This can be done through publications and airing the right teachings through the mass media.

Evolving Biblical Literacy Programmes

The church in Africa should promote biblical literacy by encouraging the reading of the Bible by ordinary people. What accounts for the gullibility of some African Christians, among other things, is biblical illiteracy. Many members of these churches do not read the Bible, and in contrast to Apostle Paul's testimony of the Berean Christians of the New Testament era: "Now these Jews were more noble than those in Thessalonica; they received the word with all eagerness, examining the Scriptures daily to see if these things were so" (Acts 17:11, ESV). There need to be a campaign of 'Back to the Bible', for

---

[18] Richard J. Gehman, *African Traditional Religion in the Light of the Bible.* Nairobi: African Christian Textbooks, 2013, [2001], pp. 3,35, 234, 246.

[19] *The Believer and Positive Confessions.* Springfield, MO: Gospel Publishing House, 1980, p. 17.

Christians and converts to read through the Bible to gain a thorough knowledge of the basics of the Christian faith and its doctrines. There should be a deliberate and consistent emphasis on the study of the Bible. There are some evangelical churches that are good at this through their Christian Education departments. For example, the Baptist denomination goes through the Bible in a three-year circle in its Sunday school.

Emphasizing the Right Building Blocks for African Christian Hermeneutics

One of the banes of African Christianity, aside from the selfish and avaricious orientation of the clergy in some settings, is the way the Bible is often interpreted. The way of reading and interpreting the Bible in this context is from the viewpoint of biblical literalism. Literal analysis means "a biblical text is to be deciphered according to the "plain meaning" expressed by its linguistic construction and historical context."[20] Many pastors who apply this method of biblical interpretation are most often susceptible to misinterpretation of the Bible. They run the risk of falling into a trap of misleading theology because they take the Bible at its face value and interpret the Bible literally. The counsel of St. Augustine may suffice in this context. Augustine underscores the meaning of diligent study of the Bible and prayers as more than human knowledge and oratory skills. He encourages the interpreter and preacher of the Bible to seek a good manner of life, and most of all to love God and their neighbour.[21] Diane Stinton, in proposing building blocks for Christological formulations in the African context, considered the articulation of Christology done in light of biblical revelation and Christian tradition, reflected in the African realities both past and present.[22]

Preaching and Affirming the Authentic Gospel

All Christians are called to be faithful witnesses of the authentic gospel of Jesus Christ, the Saviour of the world. They are to affirm the true content of the gospel wherever they find themselves. John Stott defines the gospel content as this: "The gospel is precisely this, good news of salvation or good news 'of our Saviour Christ Jesus.' Ever since the glad tidings of great joy were first announced on Christmas day in terms of the birth of 'a Saviour who is Christ the Lord' (Luke. 2:10-11), the followers of Jesus have recognized its essential

---

[20] https://www.Hermeunetics:Wikipedia.en.m.wikipedia.org. Accessed 10/10/2020
[21] Hermeneutics – *Wikipedia.org*
[22] Diane B. Stinton, *Jesus of Africa-Voices of Contemporary African Christology*, Maryknoll, NY: Orbis Books, 2006, p. 21.

content."²³ Stott affirms that first and foremost, it is the gospel of salvation; and not all the complexities that had been made out of this simple message of Christ dying for the world as the Saviour of mankind. Stott also warned that "There is only one gospel of salvation. And although both words 'gospel' and 'salvation' need today to be translated into terms meaningful to modern man, we have no liberty to alter the substance of our message."²⁴

Striving Towards a Reorientation of Authentic Christian Ethos and Values
There is no gainsaying that the flawed and unbalanced theology of the prosperity gospel skews the church's emphasis in favour of material acquisition and what adherents can benefit or achieve here and now over everything else. There has been a drift from "a message that focusses on the inheritance of heaven in the hereafter as the major motivation for calling people to Christ. It had now become one whose major emphasis is the material benefits to be gained here and now in this present life."²⁵ The liturgy and hymns in the churches changed from 'When We All Get to Heaven,' to 'Abraham's blessings are mine'. Our theology reflects on our liturgy, hymnody and lifestyle. Unfortunately, by identifying more with a worldly value system and culture, our Christianity is fast losing its saltiness and beacon of light to a sinful and morally bankrupt world. By and large, it leaves little or nothing to be desired of in Christianity.

There is an urgent need for reorientation in the ethos and values of African Christianity to reflect Christ-likeness. Christianity is essentially sacrificial. "While recognizing the blessedness of a relationship with a living, loving, caring God, they see the Christian purpose as transcending temporal blessings. The reason for being a follower of Christ extends to the giving of self, and means for the growth of God's Kingdom. A self-centred culture, the type that the neo-Pentecostal message espouses, seems to be fundamentally antithetical to the lifestyle that Jesus modelled and taught.'²⁶

Advocating for an Austere Lifestyle or Voluntary Poverty
Closely related to the above is the pursuit of asceticism as an alternative lifestyle in the midst of ravaging poverty and misery in the African context. The New Testament teaches and recommends a lifestyle of sobriety, self-denial, self-control moderation and self-discipline even in the midst of plenty. African Christians should seek to emulate Jesus Christ, who 'though he was

---

[23] John Stott, *The Message of 2 Timothy Guard The Gospel.* London: Inter-Varsity Press, 1999, p. 34.
[24] Ibid., p. 34.
[25] Gary S. Maxey & Peter Ozodo, *The Seduction of the Nigerian Church,* p. 25.
[26] Ibid., p. 29.

rich, yet for your sakes he became poor, that ye through his poverty might be rich.'(2 Corinthians 8:9). We should seek to attract and empower others who are not Christians or rich enough, through our deliberate choice of living a life of moderation in a context of a proven lack. The lavish lifestyles of some clergymen, particularly in the Pentecostal denominations, often goaded by the prosperity gospel, leaves much to be desired. Such lifestyles of opulence neither conform to the lifestyle of the founder of Christian faith, Jesus Christ, nor resonate with the experiences of the populace in Africa who are the majority poor.

Pauline's Theology of Contextualization

The prosperity gospel often does not take into consideration the suitability of this form of the gospel in the African context. While the gospel of Jesus Christ is liberating in its content, it gives consideration to the culture and lifestyle of the people where the gospel is being propagated. It is the theology of becoming as one of the people, in order to reach them for Christ. We must seek to liberate and alleviate them from an enslaving mindset through the power of the gospel, but we must adopt the prevalent culture of the people in doing so. Apostle Paul advanced the theology of becoming thus:

> And unto the Jews I became as a Jew, that I might gain the Jews; to them that are under the law, as under the law, that I might gain them that are without the law…To the weak became I as weak, that I might gain the weak: I am made all things to all men, that I might by all means save some (1 Corinthians 9:20).

This is the quintessential missionary spirit and lifestyle, espoused by none other than the stalwart of the New Testament missionary enterprise, Apostle Paul. The missionary must be seen to be living amongst the people and not above the people. The prosperity gospel advocates a lifestyle well above and beyond the reach of the people. The advocates of contextualization of the gospel argue in most cases against 'prefabricated' Christianity that hardly possesses any local content or input, but is imported whole and planted in the African context. It is a creation of a foreign culture, and has the dominant elements of foreignness in it.

As stated previously, the promotion of greed and self-centredness inadvertently by the prosperity gospel does not resonate with the majority of African cultures. Among the Zulus, for example, there is the concept of *Ubuntu*, of shared humanity, promoting a sense of common destiny and belongingness in the family, community and society at large. In effect, no one can be an island unto himself, "a person is a person through other people."[27]

---

[27] www.theguardian.com Accessed 18/11/2020

Teaching a Right Perspective on Human Suffering

The liturgical experiences in some Pentecostal churches that emphasize the prosperity gospel dwell mostly on triumphalism over life's vicissitudes. In most cases, in the course of worship, opportunities are given to members to share their testimonies, re-living their successes, achievements, accomplishments, and victories in the light of opposition and challenges. The impression given is that the Christian life is all about triumph over negative forces impinging on living a good life, and the absence of human suffering. The prosperity gospel hardly dwells on human misery, pain, suffering, and experiences of injustice in the world. The failure to reflect and identify with human misery and suffering makes the theology of the prosperity gospel to distance itself from the experiences in the African contexts, where sufferings abound. It is a contradiction to the realities on the ground in Africa, where many are enmeshed in joy-pain relationships in much of their lives. This is why the liberation theology that identifies with the poor, though tainted with the quest for grabbing political power often at the expense of the gospel, is more appealing to some in Africa who consider the prosperity gospel as strange and foreign to their life experiences.

A right perception of human weakness, failures and sufferings should be taught as part of the Christian experience as willed by God. Human sufferings serve as a crucible through which the Christian matures and attains a Christ-like disposition and character in life. Besides this, the hope of God is displayed in suffering: "We need to get rid of this idea of a 'smooth sailing God', who, when you please him, makes everything peachy keen for you."[28] That is not what Jesus' life was like, and that is not what His followers' lives are cut out to be.

Teaching Responsible Stewardship

There is the need to teach in African churches responsible stewardship as against current practices where money matters are given prominence due to the misconception and misunderstanding of the concept of stewardship. People are repeatedly asked to give over and over again as though all that matters to God is not worship, but money: "The pastors often ask the congregation to sow fatty seed so that they may reap bounteously. In the light of this, the church leaders design some offerings such as 'open offering' (the one that opens the heaven for blessings), 'poverty eradication offering' (the that removes poverty from one's life completely), and 'success offering' (the one that brings abundant and unlimited success in all earthly endeavour)."[29]

---

[28] Follow Jesus, Expect Suffering http://churchleaders.com.outreach Accessed 8/11/2020

[29] Samson Kolawole Oyeku, "African Christianity and Ecclesiastical Corruption: Nigeria as a Study Case", p. 429.

People are swindled out of their money because of their ignorance of correct Christian stewardship. The ecclesiological response should be such that Christians are made to be aware of responsible stewardship as an integral part of Christian worship. Christians are to give as an act of love, obedience and positive response to needs of expanding God's Kingdom through the propagation of the gospel of Jesus Christ. However, responsible stewardship is planned, contemplative and systematic as Apostle Paul advocated in 2 Corinthians 8 and 9. He acknowledged that the 'grace of giving 'is one of the means of grace that brings further blessings upon the Christian if done responsibly as an act of love, obedience and worship. The grace of giving demonstrates one's self-giving, exemplified by Jesus Christ who gave Himself as the ultimate sacrifice for our redemption. It is not for the purpose of self-aggrandizement or to advance one's self in terms of worldly riches as seen often in some churches of Pentecostal strands. Every church, age and particular context has had to deal with a variant or misleading theology. They abound in our world fraught with deceit, falsehood and aberrations particularly in Christian contexts or churches. It is, therefore, the responsibility of all lovers of truth to be discerning, counter the untruths, and illuminate the understanding of those who are held bondage to the half-truths and falsehoods and who are presented with a veneer masked in truth.

Christianity, Poverty and Wealth in the 21st Century Church in Africa
Modest Pesha

Conceptual Understanding of Poverty and Wealth from African and Biblical-Christian Perspectives

a. Poverty

Poverty can be defined as the collective conditions that prevent human beings from flourishing and attaining fulfillment. Poverty also is a deprivation of capabilities, empowerment and basic freedom.

b. African Perspective

The African perception of poverty differs from people in other continents. While some African social and political leaders, including Christians, assert that poverty is inevitable for the African continent, some of them strongly maintain that the 'poor are not us', and that poverty and the state of being poor have been caused by a few wealthy people through unjust and exploitative social, economic and political structures.

For African societies, it is possible to secure life and a livelihood through networking with individuals or groups within one's community. Hence, the African philosophy of life insists on having the possibilities of transforming potential, in contrast to other individualistic modes of production from Western cultures.

However, the existence of poverty in Africa is not evidence of being uncivilized which is against individualistic and materialistic biblical interpretations on poverty. Such a view is justified by the fact that the African context places more values on human beings than on material possessions, whereby the priority of the African socio-economic support system has roots in establishing social relationships for the welfare of a person. Although the continent of Africa is rich with abundant natural resources, its people continue to suffer from abject poverty because human resources and economic infrastructures are underdeveloped and controlled by people from other continents.

c. Biblical Perspective

From the biblical and Christian point of view, the Almighty God is the author, owner and provider of wealth, given to humans to be properly utilized and used for all humans: 'The earth is the Lord's and the fullness thereof, the world and those who dwell therein' (Psalm 24:2) Likewise, 'Every man to whom God has given wealth... possessions and power has to enjoy them' (Ecc 6:2). Thus, wealth and being wealthy are not evil. It becomes evil and sin when people do not want to share with other people the wealth given to them resulting in making others poor and destitute through unloving and unjust social relationships. Moreover, wealth becomes deadly when one is much wealthier than others because it leads to inequality, and separation from God and one's neighbours and, to that extent that one's wealth becomes an idol that is an object of loyalty and devotion as well as the means of oppressing others. At this juncture, unloving and unjust social relationships, poverty, oppression and subjugation become social sins.

Challenges of Poverty and Wealth to Christianity and the Church in Africa

Poverty and wealth in Africa have caused unavoidable challenges to both Christianity and the church. This is justified by the fact that any religion, like Christianity, is a key dynamic community resource for integrating, harmonizing and sustaining enduring social, economic and political transformation of livelihoods and the lives of poor people, mostly living at the grass-roots level in Africa. The lack of abundant wealth production and control of it, the lack of self-confidence and the lack of visionary leadership have ultimately resulted in the loss of a survival mechanism among the present generation of Africans.

It raises a fundamental question: in what way can Christianity make a relevant contribution to debates on contemporary socio-economic concerns related to wealth and poverty? In order to answer this question, it is important to evaluate whether Christianity and individual Christians cause poverty or contribute towards eradicating it. This could be through a prophetic voice urging African people, and especially the policy makers, to pay attention to the need of having a just and fair use of wealth.

Church Responses to the Challenge of Poverty and Wealth in Contemporary Africa

Possible answers to the question above are rooted in the fact that Christianity and the church in an African context should advocate and stand with poor people in the struggle against poverty. This is so because there are socio-economic consequences in the way we believe about the divine. It implies having an alternative popular socio-economic model, with which to enable the poor to see and understand poverty within their own context and from African perspectives. To advocate and stand with the poor is a combination of both liberation theology since pre- and post-independence and the theology of life in contemporary times. With reference to the Evangelical Lutheran Church of Tanzania (ELCT) North Western Diocese and the use of the slogan (ULIPO TUPO), meaning *where you are; there we be,* there is a pursuit of devolving church operational services closer to the people, rather than waiting for them to come once in a while, hence easily dragged into misleading theologies for miracles and false prophecies on prosperity. ULIPO TUPO is simply sending the church into the everyday life of the people, with proper teachings that lay emphasis on wealth creation and prosperity as a result of hard work as in Genesis 2:15 *"The LORD God took the man and put him in the Garden of Eden to till it and keep it."*

This kind of ongoing contemporary discussion of innovative effective methods for tackling and uprooting such an injustice in the African context, means taking on board the African culture that is akin to the ancient Israelites as a means of re-reading the sacred texts to bring forth a liberating and empowering interpretation that can transform the community. Such a contribution goes beyond the ongoing debate attempting to inquire into Christianity's equivocal understanding of poverty and transmission of the same over generations, which in Africa seems to have hurt, weakened, and failed to advance the quality of people's lives (Kimilike, 2017).

The situation of poverty and wealth in Africa demands an urgent response from the church. It demands institutions, governments and other Civic Social Organizations (CSO) in Africa to apply redemptive methods, as well as striving energetically towards acquiring and facilitating meaningful changes for the African people from existential poverty. In this regard, Jesus has to be our liberator and redeemer when he says:

> The Spirit of the Lord is upon me, because he has anointed me to preach good news to the poor. He has sent me to proclaim release to the captives and recovering of sight to the blind, to set at liberty those who are oppressed, and to proclaim the acceptable year of the Lord (Lk 4:18-19).[1]

Jesus' model allows Christians, theologians and scholars in Africa to apply liberation theology, and now a theology of life, with which to liberate and walk with both the poor and the wealthy. Being poor, and the unjust use of wealth, are contrary to the gospel of God through Jesus Christ.[2] The contemporary

---

[1] Not only giving a spiritual reflection to the biblical translations on the proclamation of release to the captives [of sin] but also on the captivity of poverty.
[2] To advocate and stand with...is a combination of both liberation theology (pre- and post-independent Africa) and the theology of life in contemporary times. See ELCT/North Western Diocese use of the 'ULIPO TUPO' slogan.

challenging economic situation, especially the fight against poverty in Africa, should engage academic biblical studies. This would involve a theological search for alternative strategies for wealth creation. It is also advisable for the church in Africa to advocate for the government to undertake controlling measures against misleading theologies resulting in unjust wealth accumulation at the expense of the poor.

Conclusion

The notion of 'the poor are not us' is a call to Africans to explain to others that they should see them the way they see and think of themselves in their struggle to eradicate poverty. However, the poor know very well that poverty solutions do not come automatically because poverty eradication is a holistic process. It is a human-centred development process that has to be undertaken through the mobilization of relationships and resources based on the traditional African socio-economic systems. Thus, eradicating or reducing poverty among the African people, mostly South of the Sahara, demands a localized initiative, which links all dimensions of human experience with the spirit of survival, that advocates a transformation of the pattern of social relationships in the process of the sensitization and mobilization of the poor. Along with this, the church could effectively air its advocating prophetic voice to letting Christians know that poverty can be eradicated when it becomes a common concern of the whole community.

Effects of Covid-19 on Wealth and Prosperity in Africa
Kwabena Asamoah-Gyadu

This section begins with a brief discussion of the effects of corona virus, before interrogating select responses of contemporary Pentecostal churches to the Covid-19 pandemic in Africa. In my recent work, *Christianity and Faith in the Covid-19 Era,* I have reflected on the fact that all the major events surrounding God's activity occurred under difficult circumstances, including lockdowns and restrictions. This is true of the Christmas story, in which Jesus and his parents were locked down in Egypt for fear of assassination, the Resurrection in which the risen Jesus revealed himself to the disciples in lockdown mode, to the day of Pentecost when they had to experience the outpouring of the Spirit in lockdown in the Upper Room.[1] Our theology of wealth and prosperity needs to be interrogated against the backdrop of these biblical experiences. Although not exclusive to them, these are the churches that are mostly associated with the preaching of the prosperity gospel. My thesis is that the outbreak of the pandemic, with its effects on social institutions, served as a reality check on the simplistic approach to prosperity and flourishing as advocated by the prosperity gospel.

The orientation towards prosperity or health-and-wealth gospel is reflected, not just in what these churches preach, but also in the public expression of faith including in their choice of names, physical structures, themes of crusades and revival meetings, and even in the personalities of their charismatic leaders, and their personal material choices. If we consider a misleading theology to be any theological teaching or outlook that is inconsistent with biblical truth as revealed and taught by Christ, then certain types of prosperity teaching would clearly fall in that category. In classifying the "prosperity gospel" as belonging to the realms of misleading theologies, I think of it not in terms of general human well-being and flourishing for that is not outside the will and purposes of God for humanity; rather, I am referring to aspects of the prosperity gospel that promise health-and-wealth for believers regardless of the will of God, and the circumstances of life. Christianity is doing well in Africa, at least in terms of numbers, but in terms of overall impact in the light of the peculiar problems of the continent, the church's approach has not been as pragmatic and decisive

---

[1] J. Kwabena Asamoah-Gyadu, *Christianity and Faith in the Covid-19 Era: Lockdown Periods from Hosanna to Pentecost.* Accra: Step Publishers, 2020.

as we see in the ways in which Jesus confronted the oppressive socio-political systems of his day.

Effects of Covid-19 on Wealth and Prosperity in Africa

The full measure of the effects of the Covid-19 pandemic will be known in the years ahead. Whether we are dealing with the current pandemic or the ones that have gone before – influenza, HIV AIDS, and Ebola – every such outbreak of a disease affects wealth and prosperity in more ways than one. In a number of these developments in which we have had to deal with pandemics, human life was hit in several ways. These include:

i. The lack of proper medical care as existing poor facilities are overstretched, with medical personnel working to save lives whilst at the same time, fearful of contracting deadly viruses;

ii. The inability to control the virus leads to the development of "ghost towns" as a result of deaths or incapacitations that keep many people locked down in their homes;

iii. The negative economic impact of the pandemic on Africa cannot be lost on us, with striking increases in both consumer prices and current account deficits that are surely going to affect standards of living. In these circumstances, the line in the Lord's prayer that says, "give us this day our daily bread," takes on an added poignancy in African contexts in which state support and welfare systems are virtually non-existent;

iv. The experiences of many African countries is that international remittances that have often kept household economically afloat have declined considerably, as migrants struggle to remit families in Africa;

v. These problems, as outlined above, have wider spatial, social, and ecological ramifications, with economically insecure groups the worst hit with the loss of jobs, a lack of medical care, and the exploitation of labour through dismissals as the pandemic comes in as a convenient excuse to lay people off.

We look towards the future in hope as the people of God were assured in Jeremiah during their painful exilic experiences (Jeremiah 29:11). The trust is that by the time we enter the post-pandemic future as we emerge out of lockdowns and restrictions, the vaccines which the rich Western scientific medical laboratories have produced would have reached the poorer economies of the global South. The politics surrounding the acquisition and distribution of the vaccines shows how the odds, in terms of dealing with the Covid-19 pandemic, are stacked against such developing economies as those of Africa. Whilst the U.S.A. and other countries in Europe are making advance payments in the acquisition of billions of vaccines, African countries have been left wondering what is going to happen to our peoples. These questions are important for very obvious reasons. We cannot revive the badly hit and damaged economic fortunes of the continent until the vaccines are available, and people and governments are able to get on with their lives. In the meantime, the only option in dealing with the socio-economic effects of the Covid-19 pandemic, humanly speaking, is to observe the non-pharmaceutical protocols that the scientific medical establishments have told us we need to adhere to if the spread of the virus is to be minimized.

A Theology of Glory and a Theology of the Cross

In non-Western contexts like ours in which religion is never left out in the search for answers, we need to resolve the tensions between prayer and flourishing as an economic endeavour. Our "help comes from the Lord, who made heaven and earth," and that is truth that Africa knows so well when it comes to confronting the realities of evil. Although speaking from a faith perspective, one cannot deny the supernatural implications of the pandemic as a source of evil, the prosperity, or health-and-wealth preaching that we interrogate here, does not properly account for this reality of evil, and the place of the cross in Christian discipleship. It has opted for what may be termed in Lutheran thought, a *theologia gloriae*, a theology of glory, to the neglect of *theologia crucis,* a theology of the cross. The theology of glory speaks a language of glory and power, things that belong to God, but the theology of the cross recognizes God in human suffering and in all that humanity considers to be weakness and foolishness. The focus on glory means the negative side of life: disappointments and agony, tragedies, health issues and financial breakdowns are problematic for contemporary Pentecostal health-and-wealth preachers. Thus, as Veli-Matti Kärkkäinen explains, Pentecostal preachers do not often tackle the problem of prayers unanswered or faith disappointed, and, as such, we rarely find in Pentecostal preaching situations in which prayers of faith were not answered the way we expect.[2]

What this means is that, in the midst of a Covid-19 pandemic that has led to the collapse of businesses, hit personal and domestic economies hard, and left world socio-economic, health and political institutions in search of answers to failure, the gospel of health-and-wealth has proven inadequate. The focus on glory and power to the neglect of the theology of the cross, has left us short in explaining the place of pain, suffering and misfortune in the lives of believers. Health-and-wealth theologies are an antithesis to the calamitous experiences that are often the lot of many ordinary African Christians. In other words, the health-and-wealth message has a very weak understanding of flourishing, as it applies to Evangelical Christian thought, in which God could tell Paul, "my

---

[2] Veli-Matti Kärkkäinen, "Theology of the Cross: A Stumbling Block to Pentecostal/Charismatic Spirituality? In Wonsuk Ma and Robert P. Menzies eds., *The Spirit and Spirituality: Essays in Honour of Russell P. Spittler.* London: T&T Clark, 2004, p. 151.

grace is sufficient for, you and my power is made perfect in weakness" (II Corinthians 12:9). It does not mean that we must willfully embrace pain and suffering, for after all, Jesus taught us to pray, "deliver us from evil." The sort of prosperity or health-and wealth mindset, which is critiqued in this presentation, tends to be a formulaic one, which approaches human flourishing through preaching that when believers confess with their lips that Jesus is Lord, and believe in their heart that with him all things are possible, they shall be. Things like poverty, lack, misfortune and calamity never happens to the Christian. The pandemic has proven that sort of preaching is very simplistic, inadequate and inconsistent with biblical truth.

I will argue that although the exercise of faith and hope in restoration must not be ruled out of our responses, reflecting on this gospel is relevant for our time in terms of its misleading worldview because much of its theological propositions have come unstuck with the strike of the Covid-19 pandemic. How did the outbreak of the pandemic affect contemporary Pentecostal/Charismatic preaching? How did the fact that the pandemic has wreaked economic, medical and emotional havoc on both believers and unbelievers alike, even forcing churches into lockdown and having to observe restrictions determine how we do Christian theology? How have the realities of evil resulting from the outbreak forced prosperity preachers to rethink their theology? These are the questions that guide the reflections that follow. In the prosperity mindset, setbacks in life, whether they express themselves in terms of a lack of material resources, natural misfortunes, failure, illness, or what is generally referred as "stagnation in life," may all be explained in terms of a lack of faith, the failure to fulfil tithing obligations, or the attack of principalities and powers on people's fortunes in life. Thus, when the pandemic struck, problematizing it in terms of a Satanic agenda against Christians and the church became a very convenient source of explanation for those in whose theology personal responsibility becomes insignificant in terms of what it means to be a believer in Christ.

Contemporary Pentecostal Churches

Contemporary Pentecostals are those new urban-centred, prosperity-preaching Charismatic movements that emerged on the African religious landscape in the last three decades of the twentieth century. They have highly influential and charismatically gifted leaders who have a public ministry because of their strong and powerful media activities that reach millions of followers around the world. It is important to note for the purposes of this presentation that belief in "Christ as the Soon Coming King", which was a central theological theme of classical Pentecostalism has all but disappeared from the messages of Charismatic pastors, but this eschatological dimension suddenly resurfaces in what was preached during the pandemic period. The leadership of the

Charismatic ministries have adopted a celebrity culture that has transformed them from ordinary pastors, to the religious equivalents of entertainment or sporting celebrities with very impressive fan bases. Their innovative use of media means that the average contemporary Pentecostal pastor may speak to wider audiences than their Sunday captive in-person audiences.

Their health-and-wealth messages of prosperity came under severe strain during the pandemic period, and challenged some of their leaders to rethink and rephrase a theological paradigm that seemed deficient of answers in the face of this crisis. At bottom, the cross of Christ has seemed more like a symbol of triumph and victory, than one of humiliation and shame. The imbalance means that Charismatic theology has often been left bereft of adequate responses in the face of evil and calamity. Pentecostalism is an experiential religion with a very forceful oral culture, and so I access the data from sermons, statements and declarations made during the lockdown period. The discussion is centred around messages delivered by some of the most important Charismatic pastors on the continent. First, the sermons and declarations were very inspirational, as they sought to bring hope to hearers through various media networks. It is important to note that these were not messages merely tailored for members of these churches. In the lockdown mode of the pandemic era, media audiences increased very significantly beyond the Sunday captive audiences of these churches. Secondly, the messages also showed how the pandemic challenged some of the triumphalist messages of prosperity that have come to be associated with this contemporary wave of Pentecostal Christianity.

Lockdown and Contemporary Pentecostal Theology
The spread of the coronavirus out of Wuhan, China, into other parts of the world hit all aspects of human life very hard, with even super-power nations scrambling for answers regarding how to deal with its effects. Communities of faith, including churches also felt the pinch as governments imposed restrictions on movements of people and public gatherings. Church meetings in Ghana, a hotbed of Charismatic Christianity, were severely hampered, but media technology came to the rescue. Charismatic Christianity, in particular, tends to centre very much on issues of power, divinely enabled prosperity, positive declarations of faith, and the principles of success and prosperity. The positive confessions and declarations based on the promises of God, for as the Archbishop Duncan-Williams said consistently in one of the messages he preached, "I am a word practitioner", meaning, I put the word of God in action in my life. In view of this very triumphalist view of the word, I was therefore keen to hear how in the face of the collapse of economics and personal fortunes, Charismatic messages were going to be reframed to address the crisis,

especially when the often-touted principles of success were now severely challenged in the face of the Covid-19 pandemic.

The materials discussed here were delivered on television and the internet and also recirculated through various social media platforms. Churches were locked down, but not locked out in terms of opportunities to listen to preaching or even participate in worship. In the face of these alternate arrangements, it was clear that the Covid-19 pandemic had, among others, challenged the faiths of many people, with Christians calling for concerted prayer to defeat a virus that some thought had been inflicted on the world by the devil. In many sermons, especially from the Charismatic sector, the coronavirus was "cursed" as demonic, an agent of the devil that was out to destroy God's people. This was particularly on account of the fact that it disrupted the nature of the church as we have come to understand it. In not a few cases, there were submissions speculating that perhaps this was the beginning of the end times, and that the second coming of Christ, the *Parousia,* which the early Pentecostals had so passionately preached about, was imminent.

One the most important biblical passages that served as the foundation of prayer in the Covid-19 period was Psalm 91. It begins with the words:

> You who live in the shelter of the Most High, who abide in the shadow of the Almighty, will say to the Lord, 'My refuge and my fortress; my God, in whom I trust' (Psalm 91:1-2).[3]

The psalmist's reference to God's deliverance from "the snare of the fowler and from the deadly pestilence" in verse 3, provided the appropriate discourse for many seeking to invoke the name and power of God in dealing with the pandemic. A lot of prayer circulating in the media used verses from this particular Psalm. Of the various Christian churches in Africa, I found the responses of the contemporary Pentecostal or Charismatic churches to the outbreak of the pandemic very instructive and revealing. This is because as churches that focus on the Charismatic experience in the power of the Holy Spirit, their theology has an interventionist orientation; they take the theology of evil seriously, and how to deal with evil features prominently in their ecclesiology.

The Covid-19 era came as a test of a situation that provided an alternative context within which to articulate Charismatic motivational messages. In the face of depressive spirits, failing businesses, empty pockets, family dislocations, sicknesses, bereavements, and so on and so forth, many, like Jesus on the cross, felt forsaken. The Pentecostal pastors seized the moment to repackage their messages on the principles of success, positives, promotion and wealth creation, to suit the spirit of the times. A number of them returned to

---

[3] All Bible quotations are from *The New Oxford Annotated Bible: New Revised Standard Version.* Oxford: Oxford University Press, 1994.

eschatological messages, a theme which many have observed had been virtually missing from Charismatic discourses. That is not to say they did not believe in judgment, hell, the Second Coming of Christ and the like. It is just that the eschatological message is simply inconsistent with the emphasis on health, wealth and material prosperity that had become part of the charismatic self-definition in terms of religious emphasis. Whether articulated in terms of the power of Jesus or that of the Holy Spirit, Charismatic Christianity speaks the language of power in which God turns impossibilities into possibilities.

Covid-19 as a Reality Check

The depressive circumstances that the Covid-19 pandemic situation created, offered the virtual perfect fit for the sort of motivational and inspiring messages associated with contemporary Pentecostalism. Its prosperity message had often sounded a bit monolithic and myopic in the sense that, although it is preached in full knowledge that suffering and evil are real, those sorts of circumstances have often been ignored. I have argued elsewhere that the emphasis on the power of triumph, success, promotion, life, health, victory and overcoming, had blinded many preachers to the real-life circumstances of their patrons. These messages were simply confronted with a reality check in the midst of the Covid-19 pandemic. It is the triumphal stories of those who are winning that we often hear about in testimonies, with those going through challenges often treated as if they do not apply the right principles of success, which would usually mean the faithful fulfillment of tithing obligations.

In contrast to the regular messages that those who fulfil certain religious obligations would be successful and win the battles of life, this particular demon – the corona virus – was affecting the fortunes of everyone, including pastors and prophets who had assured us that faithful Christians were beyond the logic of suffering. Many took to social media to question the inability of the African Charismatic prophets to foretell the onset of the corona virus, and if not deal with it, at least, get the world to prepare for this onslaught of evil. The world was locked down through the Passion week, Easter and Pentecost. The lockdowns did not afford Pentecostal pastors the usual opportunities to advertise their triumphalist themes such as "the benefits of the cross", "the blood that speaks", or the "power of the resurrection". Here, for instance, is a selection of a combination of prayer and declarations made by Archbishop Nicholas Duncan-Williams in the early weeks of the pandemic:

> The Coronavirus is a name, is a person without body and in the name of Jesus, as we bow our knee and we pray, in the name of Jesus, this plague, pestilence and virus will bow the knee and will stand down and go back from whence it came in the name of Jesus. The Lord is good, a strong hold in the day of trouble and he knows them that trust in Him. I challenge you, within these thirty days to trust in the Lord like never before. Show the enemy that your faith is in God. If we only

trust God when everything is good and in good times when everything is alright, then it is not faith and it is not trust. But it is the times of trouble and moments like this that we know whether we trust God, or we don't trust God. It is times like this that your faith and my faith is renewed, it takes times like this, trying situations like this, to reveal the strength of our faith. Trust in God, I challenge you to trust in God, to have faith in God, as never before.

The Archbishop proceeds to assure his hearer to ignore the apocalyptic readings that many were putting into the rise of the pandemic:

This is not the end of the world, there are people who are saying that this virus is judgment from God, and that it is the sign of the end of the world. They are entitled to their opinion. And others believe it is from the enemy, but whatever these schools of thoughts are, it doesn't bother me. The most important thing is for you to have right standing with God, because if you have a right standing with God, if it is from the enemy, the Bible says "no weapon formed against you shall prosper, and every tongue that rises in judgment against you, shall be condemned. And if it is judgment from God, in the Day of Judgment, God has promised to deliver and to exempt His chosen, His children, from the judgment. So, whatever it is, you are covered. And I don't want you to entertain fear, don't entertain any fear because the blood of Jesus has covered us, the Bible said "when I see the blood, when I see the blood, when I see the blood, I will pass over you."

In response to the pandemic, he proceeded to invoke the power of the blood of Jesus to deal with its effects:

We invoke the blood of Jesus over this nation, we invoke the blood of Jesus over our borders, our airwaves, our high seas and the land, and every family of this country and nation and all the members of our church. We invoke the blood of Jesus that this virus and this angel of death will pass over our dwellings, will pass over our loved ones, will pass over all that concerns us and that there will be no loss of any father, mother, wife, husband, boy or girl or grandson or granddaughter. There will be no loss of any life among us, and that our wives will not be widows, and our children will not be fatherless. And no father or mother will bury their children by any means in the name Jesus…In the face of adversity, in the face of disaster and in the face of tragedy, you are an overcomer.

As with the first Passover and the first Crucifixion and Resurrection days in the Bible, everyone was locked down, and although the messages were still empowering, preachers were challenged by the circumstances to tweak them a bit in order to account for what the world was going through.

Reframing the Health-and-Wealth Gospel

Until the Covid-19 pandemic outbreak, one would have struggled to hear sermons on the Second Coming of Christ among contemporary Pentecostal preachers. I have argued elsewhere that one scarcely hears sermons about eschatological events in a contemporary Charismatic world. This is because, a preacher cannot encourage members to make as much money as they could, build big and palatial homes, buy the best in luxurious cars, and at the same time preach that, but anyway, Jesus could appear like a thief in the night.[4] Contemporary Pentecostals believe in God's end-time judgment and the Second Coming of Christ, but they simply do not preach it. Paul Gifford also mentions this in his book, *Ghana's New Christianity,* noting that the recurring emphasis in this form of Christianity "has to do with success, wealth and status."[5] If these are the recurring themes of contemporary Pentecostalism, what changed in the first quarter of the year 2020?

Prosperity preachers were forced to respond to a pandemic that revealed the realities of life. In the period of the corona virus consternation, there was certainly a change in mood, and several preachers took on eschatological issues that had hitherto been placed on the back burner. Archbishop Nicholas Duncan-Williams, whilst invoking the blood upon people, at the same time, had claimed on Palm Sunday that this was a wake-up call for the church to realize that "we have a place to go." The reason for the born-again experience was for us to prepare for eternity, he noted. In his words: "this is the time for purity, holiness, righteousness in heart and motive; this is not the time to make money but to give and be a child of God like never before. This is not the time to bear grudges." These "worldly things" would be obstacles when Jesus returns to judge the world." This new emphasis was a complete antithesis to his proposals in the book *"You Are Destined to Succeed",* in which the Archbishop claimed that the use of luxurious material things were divine rights and not options for "a man of God."[6]

On the Sunday of the Triumphal Entry, Archbishop Duncan-Williams preached on the works of the flesh (I Thessalonians 5:2-3). "This is the time for people to get saved…if we do not get into the ark now, we will be left behind." This corona virus is a "pestilence and a plague", he noted. The only thing that can save humanity is to get into the ark of our salvation, which is Christ. It was instructive to hear Archbishop Duncan-Williams saying people must "endure" trials and temptations. All the prophecies are falling into place, he further noted, for the Son of Man is coming again. He refers to Matthew 24:22, "And if those days had not been cut short, no one would be saved; but for the sake of the elect, those days would be cut short."

The point was that in the Covid-19 situation, we have seen nations evacuate their citizens. It is the same way in which "heaven will evacuate its own", that

---

[4] J. Kwabena Asamoah-Gyadu, *Sighs and Signs of the Spirit: Ghanaian Perspectives on Pentecostalism and Renewal in Africa.* Oxford: Regnum, 2015, pp. 163-176.
[5] Paul Gifford, *Ghana's New Christianity,* p. 44.
[6] Nicholas Duncan-Williams, *You are Destined to Succeed.* Accra: Action Faith Publications, 1990.

is, the elect, at the imminent return of Jesus: "God will send an aircraft with Jesus as its captain, and every believer will be evacuated home." He explained that only "citizens of heaven" would qualify for the evacuation, and made a direct appeal in his broadcast for listeners who did not know Jesus to embrace him as Lord and Saviour. The days of suffering would be shortened for the sake of the elect, he emphasized. God said, "I will spare the elect", and so, all the citizens of heaven will be evacuated; you cannot go the airport if America sends an aircraft to evacuate her citizens if you do not have an American passport; even your spouse, if they are American would be evacuated and you will be left behind; the rapture is an aircraft," the Archbishop noted.

I was struck by the terms and expressions that were deployed in this thoroughly eschatological message: heaven, hell, redeemed, sanctification, preparedness, purity, uprightness, rapture, and these as compared to the recurring emphasis on material success that Gifford talks about. Archbishop Duncan-Williams concluded with the story of the virgins (Matthew 25:1-13). At the announcement of the arrival of the bridegroom, only those with adequate oil in their lamps were able to meet him. In the same way, "if you are not a citizen of a country, it does not matter who you are married to, you will not be evacuated when the rapture takes place." It was striking because this is a preacher, who like many others in his category, often centred his sermons on tithing and offerings as seed-sowing for blessing; wealth, health, and upward mobility as the right of the Christian. "This is not the time to make money" the Archbishop said, rather, "this is the day to show compassion; you can have all the money in the world, but it cannot save you; a day is coming when all these material things will mean nothing." What the tensions between what was previously preached in health-and-wealth, and what is happening with the pandemic is that Pentecostal/Charismatic Christians ought to make sure that they are equipped to come to grips with the inevitable questions of life: the existence of suffering, the duality of human faith, the mystery of God's hiddenness, the ultimate fate of all humans, and that is, death, and the role of faith in all these experiences.[7]

Conclusion

In the midst of the pandemic, people who were preaching about visas and international travel as a means of prosperity suddenly found the space in these times to talk about the issues of heaven and hell. Many focused on pragmatic ways of dealing with the economic and health crises that we identified at the beginning of this presentation. These two major examples from Charismatic preaching within the Covid-19 period shows how circumstances, contexts and the unpredictability of the future can affect one's understanding of church, and

---

[7] Kärkkäinen, "Theology of the Cross," p. 151.

the message that is carried in the name of Jesus Christ. On the one hand, we see how the corona virus situation led to the preaching of very pragmatic sermons that confront evil as an existential reality. On the other hand, we see from Archbishop Duncan-Williams, how the realities of evil leads to a rethinking of a gospel that had become so materialistic, that the things of eternity had been dislodged from their central place in contemporary Charismatic ecclesiology.

The eschatological messages of the Covid-19 era resonate very much with what happened to one of the apostles of the prosperity gospel, Jim Baker, who after his fall from grace due to imprisonment for federal crimes, returned to write a very instructive book, *Prosperity and the Coming Apocalypse,* in which he denounces his earlier message that materialism was a prime indicator of God's favour. The messages of prosperity preached by contemporary Pentecostal pastors are not entirely unbiblical, for there is such a thing as biblical prosperity (Psalm 1; John 10:10). And indeed, the born-again experience itself has in the lives of many people led to both a redemptive uplift in both its spiritual and material senses. When the born-again convert from lives of worldliness, vanity and carnality, critical material resources become available for constructive uses, and investments in personal and family lives are enhanced.

What we criticize is, therefore, not material prosperity as part of God's blessing, but the fact that materialism – the love of money – is the root of all evil. Besides, the materialistic gospel of prosperity fails to account for existential evil, and those whose lives are impacted by it are left without answers regarding their afflictions. Many of the principles of prosperity, as I have argued, come unstuck in the face of misfortune, calamity and evil, and the hope is that the corona virus has, among other things, exposed the areas of deficiency. It is to that end that I call aspects of the prosperity gospel misleading. This is a call for things to be rectified using the very biblical resources that are used to justify what it means to prosper in an uncertain world, in which everything else is temporal, and God alone remains sovereign. When we defer to His wisdom, we will walk through the valley of the shadow of death and still fear no evil because God is with His people.

Bibliography

Abebe, Abebaw, 'The Key Challenges of Youth in Ethiopia,' *Journal of Agricultural Economics and Rural Development*, 2009.

Altena, Thorsten, "Missionare und Einheimische Gesellschaft: Zur Kulturbegegnung der Bethel- Mission in Deutsch-Ostafrika 1890-1916." In Matthias Benad (ed.) *Bethel Mission (1): Zwischen Epileptischenpflege und Heidenbekehrung: Beiträge zur Westfälischen Kirchengeschichte.*

Anderson Allan H., "Pentecostalism." In *Global Dictionary of Theology*. ed. William A., Dyrness et al. Nottingham: Inter-Varsity Press, 2008.

_____ 'The newer Pentecostal and Charismatic Churches: The shape of Future Christianity in Africa?' *Pneuma* 24, No 2. Fall, 2002, pp. 167-184.

Arén, Gustav, *Envoys of the Gospel in Ethiopia: In the Steps of the Evangelical Pioneers 1898-1936*. Studia Missionalia Upsaliensia LXXV. Stockholm: EFS, 1999.

Asamoah–Gyadu, J. Kwabena, *Contemporary Pentecostal Christianity: Interpretation from an African Context*. Eugene, OR: Wipf and Stock 2013.

_____ "Essential Features of Misleading theologies in Africa". In *Addressing Contextual Misleading Theologies in Africa Today*. (ed.) Bosela E Eale and Njoroge J. Ngige. Oxford: Regnum Books International, 2020, pp. 12-43.

Ayantayo, J. K. "*Prosperity Gospel and Social Morality: A Critique.*" In *Creativity and Change in Nigeria Christianity*. David Ogungbile and Akintunde Akinade (eds.) Lagos: Malthouse Press, 2017, p. 203.

Aylward, S. & Njiru, J. N. *New Religious Movements in Africa*. Nairobi: Pauline Publications Africa, 2001.

Balcomb, A. O., "African Theology, Evangelical, Contextual." In *Global Dictionary of Theology*, William A. Dyrness and Veil-Matti Kärkkäinen (eds.) Nottingham: Inter-Varsity Press, 2008, pp. 7-10.

Bakke Johnny, *Christian Ministry: Patterns and Functions within the Ethiopian Evangelical Church Mekane Yesus*. Studia Missionalia Upsalinsia xliv. Oslo: Solum Forlag A.S., 1987.

Barrett, David B. *World Christian Encyclopaedia*. Nairobi: Oxford University Press, 1982, p. 660.

Barron, Bruce, *The Health and Wealth Gospel: What is Going on Today in a Movement that has shaped the faith of millions?* Downers Grove, IL: Inter Varsity Press, 1987.

Benad, Matthias, "Einleitung." In Matthias Benad (ed.) *Bethel Mission (1): Zwischen Epileptischenpflege und Heidenbekehrung: Beiträge zur Westfälischen Kirchengeschichte.*

Bible. *La Bible avec notes d'étude, Vie nouvelle, Segond 21.* Romanel-sur-Lausanne: Société Biblique de Genève 2009, p. 260.

Biema van, David and Jeff Chu 'Does God Want You to Be Rich?' *Time*, 2006.

Bowler, K. *Blessed: A history of the American prosperity gospel.* Oxford: Oxford University Press, 2013.

Brouwer, S., Gifford P., & Rose, S. D. *Exporting the American gospel: Global Christian fundamentalism*. New York: Routledge, 1996.

Bulutse, Futuwi, *An Introduction to the Theology and Growth of Independent Churches in Ethiopia with Special Reference to Rema Faith Church: A critical Approach.* EGST, Unpublished M.Th. Thesis, 2002.

Buys, Filp, *Paying Unpaid Debts. Reformational Antidotes for Some of the Challenges Posed by Prosperity Gospel Theology.*

Carfantan, J. Y., *Vaincre la faim, c'est possible.* Paris: Seuil, 1983.

Carpenter, Joel and Nellie Kooistra, *Engaging Africa: Report.* New York: Nagel Institute of Calvin College, 2014.

Cochrane, James, John de Cruchy and Robin Petersen, *In Word and Deed, Towards A Practical Theology for Social Transformation.* Pietermaritzburg: Cluster Publications, 1991.

Cohen, L., Manion, L., & Morrison, K., *Research methods in education.* 6th ed. New York: Routledge, 2013.

Copeland, Kenneth, *The Laws of Prosperity.* Tulsa: Harrison House, 1974.

Dawson, Christopher, *Progress and Religion: An historical enquiry into the Causes and Development of the Idea of Progress and its Relationship to Religion.* New York: Image Books, 1960.

Djanie, A. 'Losing my Soul,' *New African,* No. 503, February, 2011, p. 35.

Eglises luthériennes. *La foi des Eglises luthériennes: Confessions et catéchismes.* Textes édités par André Birmelé et Marc Lienhard. Paris: Editions du Cerf, 1991.

Ekebbuisi, Chinonyerem Chijioke. 'Colonial Power, Garrick Braide and the Campaign Against

Liquor Trade that devalues Moral, Ethical and Spiritual Foundation for Prosperous Nigeria,' *Journal of West African Association of Theological Institutions, Politics and the Church in Africa,* pp. 85-107.

Ela, J. M., *L'Afrique des villages.* Paris: Karthala, 1982.

Ethiopia. The Federal Republic of Ethiopian Ministry of Youth, Sports and Culture, 2004.

Fekadu Gurmesa, *Evangelical Faith Movement in Ethiopia: Origins and Establishment of the Ethiopian Evangelical Church Meakne Yesus.* Minneapolis, MN: Lutheran University Press, 2009.

Ferguson, Sinclair B. et al. (eds.) *New Dictionary of Theology.* Leicester: Inter-Varsity Press, 1989.

Fihavango, G, M. *Vita dhidi ya umasikini: Imani na Ujasiriamali.* 2015, pp. 64-71.

FLM. *Donne-nous aujourd'hui notre pain quotidien, Onzième Assemblée Générale de la FLM, Matériel d'Etude, Deuxième jour, 2007.*

Gay, L. R., Mills, Geoffrey, E. & Airasien, Peter, A., *Educational research: competencies for Analysis and Applications.* 10th ed. Hoboken, NJ: Pearson Education, 2012.

Gerard, André-Marie «*Elyôn.*» In *Dictionnaire de la Bible.* Paris: Robert Laffont, 1989, p. 321.

Gifford, Paul, *Ghana's New Christianity: Pentecostalism in a globalizing African economy.* Bloomington, IN: Indiana University Press, 2004.

Goliama, Castor Michael, "The Gospel of Prosperity in African Pentecostalism: A Theological and Pastoral Challenge to the Catholic Church – with Reference to the Archdiocese of Songea, Tanzania." Ph.D. Dissertation, 2013.

Gwimi, Samuel P., 'The Significance of African Spirituality in the realization of Vision 2063.' *Journal of West African Association of Theological Institutions, Politics and the Church in Africa,* 2017, pp. 136-156.

Hall, Douglas John 'What is Theology?' *Cross Currents,* 25, no. 2, 2003.

Holland, Joe and Peter Henriot, S.J., *Social Analysis: Linking Faith and Justice.* Maryknoll, NY: Orbis Books, 1984.
Hamidou, Kane Cheikh, *L'Aventure Ambigüe.* Paris:Union Générale des Editions, 1961.
Heuser1, Andreas 'Charting African Prosperity Gospel.' Teologiese Studies/Theological Studies.
Holter, Knut (ed.) *Interpreting Classical Religious Texts in Contemporary Africa.* Nairobi: Action Publishers, 2007, pp. 105-117, 165-180.
Horton, M., *The agony of deceit.* Chicago, IL: Moody Press, 1990, p. 28.
Jäger, Alfred, *Diakonie als christliches Unternehmen: Theologische Wirtschaftsethik im Kontextdiakonischer Unternehmenspolitik. 4 Auflage. Gütersloh: Gürtersloher Verlagshaus Gerd Mohn, 1993.*
_____ *Wirtschaftsethik als ökonomisches und christliches Postulat.* Nürnberg, 1989.
Jones, D. W., "The Bankruptcy of the prosperity Gospel: An Exercise in Biblical and Theological Ethics", 2006 https:/bible.org/article/bankruptcy-prosperity-gospel-exercise-biblical-and-theological-ethics, retrieved 20/10/2020.
Kalu O., "African Theology, Protestant." In *Global Dictionary of Theology,* ed. by William A. Dyrness and Veil-Matti Kärkkäinen. Nottingham: Inter-Varsity Press, 2008, pp. 10-15.
Keshomshahara, Abednego , *A Theology of Poverty Reduction in Tanzania: A Quest for Socio- Economic and Political Vision.* Dodoma: CTP, 2008.
Keshomshahara, 'Kazi za Roho Mtakatifu na Changamoto za Siku hizi.' In *Semina ya Kiroho: Maombi,Miujiza naKazi za Roho Mtakatifu dhidi ya Changamoto za hizi.* Mwanza: Godwin Gunewe Publishers, 2017.
Kimilike, P. L. (ed.) 'Poverty context in Proverbs 31:1-9: A Bena Tanzanian analysis for Transformational Leadership Training.' *OTE* 31 no. 1 (2018):pp. 135-163. https://doi.org/10.17159/2312-3621/2018/v31n1a8
Ki-Zerbo, Joseph, *Histoire de l'Afrique noire. Paris:* Hatier, 1978.
_____ «L'influence des modèles culturels occidentaux sur les sociétés africaines.» In *Flambeau Spécial Education,* Nos. 34-35, mai-août, 1972, pp. 95-108.
Koch, B. A. 'Who Are the Prosperity Gospel Adherents?' *Journal of Ideology,* 2014, p. 36. An electronic journal at: www.lsus.edu/journalofideology.
Koch, Bradley, "The Prosperity Gospel and Economic Prosperity: Race, Class, Giving, and Voting." Ph.D. Thesis, Indiana University, 2009.
Lausanne Theology Working Group Statement on the Prosperity Gospel, *Evangelical Review of Theology* 34, 3, 2010, pp. 99-102.
Leith, J. H., *Crisis in the Church: The Plight of Theological Education.* Louisville, KY, Westminster John Knox, 1997.
Lindhardt, M. "Miracle Makers and Money Takers: Healers, Prosperity Preachers and Fraud in Contemporary Tanzania." In Amanda van Eck (ed.) *In Good Faith: Minority Religions and Fraud.* Aldershot: Ashgate, 2012, pp. 153–180.
Mabounda, François, *L'erghotheologie: Une doctrine biblique du travail.* Yaoundé, Editions Clé, 2018, p. 147.
Macdonald, William, Fastard Arthur, *Le commentaire biblique Ancien Testament du disciple.* Romanel-sur-Lausanne: Société Biblique de Genève, 2010, p. 194.
Mahali, Faustine, *The Concept of Poverty in Luke from the Perspective of the Wanji of Tanzania.* Arusha: Makumira, 2006.
Makulilo, Alexander. '"You must only drink one cup": Revisiting the tension between "Kikombe cha Babu" and biomedicine in Tanzania.' In *The African Review,* v. 45. Number 2, 2018.
Martin, D., *Pentecostalism: The World Their Parish.* Oxford: Blackwell, 2002, p. 28.

McConnell, D. R. *A different gospel: A historical and biblical analysis of the modern Faith Movement*. Peabody, MA: Hendrickson Publishers, 1988.

Mekane Yesus. The 2019 Statistic of the Ethiopian Evangelical Church Mekane Yesus, Unpublished, Addis Ababa.

Mndeme, A. Danga, "Gemeindediakonie" (Diakonenschule Nazareth Fachseminar für Gemeindepflege, Bethel, 15 June, 1983).

Nihinlola, Emiola. *Integrated Theology and Pastoral Ministry in Africa*. Bangalore: Theological Trust, 2011.

_____*Theology Under the Mango Tree: A Handbook of African Theology*. Lagos: Print & Manufacturing, 2013.

Niwagila, Wilson, *From the Catacomb to a Self-Governing Church: A Case Study of the African Initiative and the Participation of the foreign missions in the Mission History of the North Western Diocese of the Evangelical Lutheran Church in Tanzania 1890-1965*, 2nd ed., Hamburg: Verlag an der Lottbek, 1991.

Nürnberg, Klaus, *Christi and the Ancestors in a changing Africa: The Living Dead and the Living God.* Pietermaritzburg: Cluster Publications, 2007.

Ojo, M.A. D*iscovering the Other Side: Challenges of Other Religions* ed. Emiola Nihinlola and Mojisola Olaniyan. Ibadan: Flourish Books, 2004.

O'Donovan,Wilbur, *Biblical Christianity in African Perspective*. Carlisle: Paternoster Press, 1996.

_____*Biblical Christianity in Modern Africa*. Carlisle: Paternoster Press, 2000.

Packer, James I., *Knowing God: With Study Guide*. London: Hodder & Stoughton. 1993.

Patte, Daniel (ed.) *The Cambridge Dictionary of Christianity*, Cambridge: Cambridge University Press, 2010, pp. 522-551; 922-999; 1299-1302.

Penoukou E. J., *Eglises d'Afrique: Propositions pour l'avenir*. Paris: Karthala, 1984.

Poswick R.-Ferdinand, Rainotte Guy (eds.), *Élyôn*, in: *Dictionnaire de la Bible et des 3 religions du Livre*. Paris: Lidis, 1985, p. 170.

Robbins, J., 'The Globalization of Pentecostal and Charismatic Christianity.' In *Annual Review of Anthropology*, 33, 2004, pp. 121.

Roser, Traugott, and Zitt, Renate "Vom Monolog zum Dialog, von soziale Tat zu Ordnung: zur Beziehung zwischen Theologie und Oekonomie" in Daniel Dietzfelbinger and Jochen Teuffel (eds.) *Heils-Okonomie:Zum zusammenwirken von Kirche und Wirtschaft*. Guetersloh: Chr. Kaiser Guetehrsloher Verlagshaus, 2002.

Sauvetre, Miche, «Des Ecoles, pourquoi faire?» *Flambeau Spécial Education*, Nos 34-35, mai-août, 1972.

Stott, J., *Understanding the Bible*. Grand Rapids, MI: Baker Books, 1984, pp. 226-227.

Tariku, Tolosa, *The Place and Purpose of Spiritual Gifts in the Scripture: The Understanding of the EECMY IBS Congregations in Mettu and Alge Towns*. Doctoral Dissertation, Concordia Theological Seminary, Fort Wayen, 2019.

Tibebe, Eshete, *The Evangelical Movement in Ethiopia*. Waco, TX: Baylor University Press, 2009.

Wagner, C. Peter, *Churchquake!* Ventura, CA: Regal Books, 1999.

Wood, Charles M., *An Invitation to Theological Study*. Valley Forge, PA: Trinity Press International, 1994.

World Council of Churches. *Christian Faith and World Economy Today: A Study Document from the WCC*. Geneva: WCC 1992.

Yamini Narayanan, 'Religion and Sustainable Development: Analysing the Connections', *Sustainable Development* 21, 2013, pp. 131-139.